Canon EOS R5 Mark II Handbook for Beginners

The Key to Capturing Stunning Photography

Rute Terra

Copyright © 2024 **RuteTerra**

This book or parts thereof may not be reproduced in any form, stored in any retrieval system, or transmitted in any form by any means—electronic, mechanical, photocopy, recording, or otherwise—without prior written permission of the publisher, except as provided by United States of America copyright law and fair use.

Disclaimer and Terms of Use

The author and publisher of this book and the accompanying materials have used their best efforts in preparing this book. The author and publisher make no representation or warranties with respect to the accuracy, applicability, fitness, or completeness of the contents of this book. The information contained in this book is strictly for informational purposes. Therefore, if you wish to apply the ideas contained in this book, you are taking full responsibility for your actions.

Printed in the United States of America

TABLE OF CONTENTS

TABLE OF CONTENTS III

CHAPTER 1 1

INTRODUCTION TO CANON EOS R5 MARK II 1

    Overview of Key Features 1
    Differences Between the R5 and R5 Mark II 5
    Who is this Camera For? (Beginners vs. Professionals) 9

CHAPTER 2 14

GETTING STARTED WITH THE R5 MARK II 14

    Unboxing and Setting Up the Camera 14
    Basic Menu Navigation and Customization 26
    Understanding Battery and Storage Options 31

CHAPTER 3 38

MASTERING PHOTOGRAPHY MODES 38

    Auto and Scene Modes for Beginners 38
    Manual, Aperture, and Shutter Priority Modes 43
    Using Bulb Mode and Advanced Settings for Professionals 50

CHAPTER 4 56

AUTOFOCUS AND EXPOSURE CONTROL 56

    Autofocus System Overview and Settings 56
    The Exposure Triangle: ISO, Shutter Speed, and Aperture 61
    Metering Modes and Exposure Compensation 65

CHAPTER 5 72

WORKING WITH LENSES 72

    Lens Compatibility: RF vs. EF Lenses 72
    Focusing Techniques for Sharp Images 77
    Using Lens Accessories (Filters, Hoods, Extenders) 82

CHAPTER 6 90

SHOOTING STILL PHOTOGRAPHY 90

    High-Resolution Image Capture and RAW Shooting 90
    Burst Shooting and High-Speed Photography 94
    Creative Shooting: HDR, Multiple Exposure, and Bracketing 98

CHAPTER 7 103

VIDEO RECORDING CAPABILITIES 103

8K and 4K Video Recording Options on the Canon EOS R5 Mark II 103
Frame Rates, Resolutions, and Formats on the Canon EOS R5 Mark II 106
Audio Settings and External Microphone Use on the Canon EOS R5 Mark II 110

CHAPTER 8 118

ADVANCED FEATURES FOR PROFESSIONALS 118

Dual Pixel RAW: Editing Flexibility 118
What is In-Body Image Stabilization (IBIS)? 122
Focus Stacking and Advanced Image Processing 128

CHAPTER 9 133

WIRELESS CONNECTIVITY AND SHARING 133

Wi-Fi and Bluetooth Pairing for Remote Control 133
Transferring Images via Canon Camera Connect App 139
Cloud Storage and Image Sharing Options 143

CHAPTER 10 150

MAINTENANCE AND TROUBLESHOOTING 150

Cleaning and Caring for Your Camera and Lenses 150
Firmware Updates and Camera Calibration 154
Troubleshooting Common Issues and Errors 159

GLOSSARY 165

CHAPTER 1

INTRODUCTION TO CANON EOS R5 MARK II

Overview of Key Features

The Canon EOS R5 Mark II is one of the most advanced mirrorless cameras available today, designed to cater to both beginners and professionals. It builds on the success of the original EOS R5, offering enhanced features and technological advancements that make it a powerful tool for photographers and videographers. In this section, we'll explore the key features of the Canon EOS R5 Mark II, breaking them down in simple terms for better understanding.

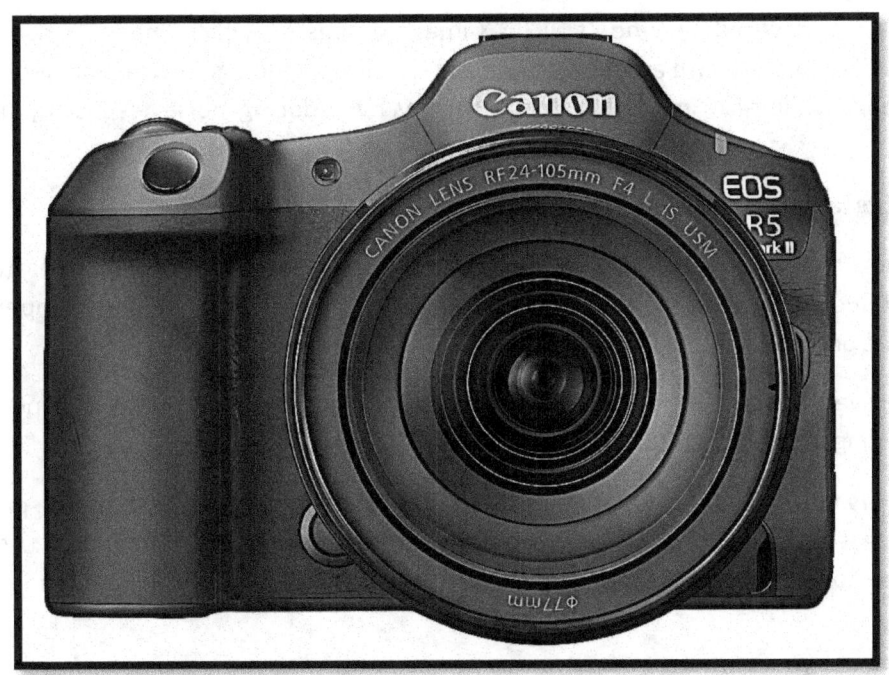

1. 45 Megapixel Full-Frame Sensor

The heart of the Canon EOS R5 Mark II is its 45-megapixel full-frame sensor. This sensor captures an extraordinary amount of detail, making it ideal for photographers who want to print large photos or crop images without losing clarity. The large sensor size also improves low-light performance, allowing you to shoot in darker environments while maintaining high image quality.

Why It's Important:

- **High Resolution**: With 45 megapixels, the R5 Mark II can capture intricate details in every shot. Whether you're photographing landscapes, portraits, or products, the resolution allows you to create crisp, clear images.
- **Low-Light Capability**: A full-frame sensor is larger than sensors in typical consumer cameras, meaning it can gather more light. This helps reduce noise and grain in your images, especially in dimly lit conditions.

How Beginners Can Use It: Beginners can benefit from the high resolution by experimenting with cropping and learning how to preserve image quality. The improved low-light performance also makes it easier to shoot in a variety of conditions without worrying too much about lighting.

2. DIGIC X Image Processor

The R5 Mark II is powered by Canon's DIGIC X image processor, which enhances overall camera performance. The processor plays a crucial role in speeding up image processing, autofocus, and burst shooting, while also improving image quality by reducing noise, especially at high ISO settings.

Why It's Important:

- **Faster Performance**: The DIGIC X processor allows the camera to shoot faster, both in continuous shooting mode (up to 20 frames per second) and in general operation, like image preview and playback.
- **Improved Image Quality**: The processor helps reduce noise in photos, especially when shooting in low-light situations or at higher ISO settings.

How Beginners Can Use It: Beginners will notice that the camera feels fast and responsive. You can capture fast-moving subjects, like kids playing or pets running, without any lag. Additionally, the improved noise reduction makes it easier for newcomers to shoot in less-than-ideal lighting conditions.

3. 8K Video Recording

One of the standout features of the Canon EOS R5 Mark II is its ability to record 8K video. This is an extremely high video resolution, offering four times the detail of 4K. The 8K video recording feature is perfect for professionals who need high-quality footage for film production, as well as content creators looking to future-proof their work.

Why It's Important:

- **Incredible Detail**: 8K resolution captures fine details, making it ideal for professional videographers who need the highest quality footage.

- **Creative Flexibility**: When editing 8K video, you can crop and zoom without losing quality, which gives you more creative options when framing your shots.

How Beginners Can Use It: Although beginners may not immediately need 8K resolution, learning to work with such high-quality video can be a great way to future-proof your content. Even if you downscale to 4K or 1080p, starting with 8K footage ensures that your videos will look sharp and professional for years to come.

4. Dual Pixel CMOS Autofocus II

The autofocus system in the R5 Mark II is one of the most advanced on the market. Canon's Dual Pixel CMOS AF II provides fast and accurate autofocus across the entire frame, with 100% coverage of the image sensor. It also offers eye, face, and animal detection, ensuring that your subject stays sharp even in fast-moving or unpredictable situations.

Why It's Important:

- **Accurate Focusing**: The Dual Pixel CMOS AF II system locks onto subjects quickly and accurately, even in challenging lighting conditions or when dealing with moving subjects.
- **Subject Tracking**: With eye, face, and animal detection, the camera can track your subject with ease, keeping them in focus no matter where they move within the frame.

How Beginners Can Use It: For beginners, the autofocus system takes the guesswork out of focusing. Whether you're shooting portraits, pets, or wildlife, you can rely on the camera to track and focus on the subject automatically, allowing you to focus on composition and creativity instead of technical settings.

5. In-Body Image Stabilization (IBIS)

The Canon EOS R5 Mark II features 8 stops of in-body image stabilization (IBIS), which helps reduce blur from camera shake when shooting handheld. This feature is especially beneficial in low-light situations or when using slower shutter speeds. It also works with Canon's RF lenses, providing even more stabilization when combined with lens-based stabilization systems.

Why It's Important:

- **Sharper Images**: IBIS compensates for small movements when shooting handheld, ensuring sharper images, especially in low-light conditions.
- **Smooth Video**: For videographers, IBIS provides smoother handheld footage, reducing the need for external stabilizers or gimbals.

How Beginners Can Use It: Beginners will appreciate the ability to shoot sharp photos without always needing a tripod. If you're shooting in low light or using slower shutter speeds, IBIS will help keep your images free from blur caused by camera shake.

6. Dual Memory Card Slots

The R5 Mark II comes with two memory card slots: one for CFexpress cards and another for SD UHS-II cards. CFexpress cards are extremely fast and are recommended for shooting 8K video or high-speed bursts, while SD cards are more affordable and widely available.

Why It's Important:

- **Flexible Storage**: Dual card slots allow you to use two cards simultaneously, either as a backup (for redundancy) or to store different types of files (e.g., RAW on one card and JPEG on the other).
- **Fast Data Transfer**: The CFexpress slot enables super-fast writing speeds, ensuring that the camera can handle large files like 8K video without delay.

How Beginners Can Use It: Beginners can use the SD card slot for day-to-day shooting, but as you advance and start shooting more video or high-resolution photos, the CFexpress slot will be useful for managing larger files quickly.

7. High-Speed Continuous Shooting

The Canon EOS R5 Mark II offers impressive continuous shooting speeds, capable of capturing up to 20 frames per second (fps) with the electronic shutter or 12 fps with the mechanical shutter. This feature is invaluable for action photographers, wildlife photographers, or anyone trying to capture fast-moving subjects.

Why It's Important:

- **Capture Every Moment**: High-speed shooting allows you to capture multiple frames per second, increasing your chances of getting the perfect shot in fast-paced situations.
- **Ideal for Action**: Whether you're photographing sports, wildlife, or any fast-moving scene, the ability to shoot at 20 fps ensures you won't miss critical moments.

How Beginners Can Use It: For beginners, this feature can be helpful when learning how to photograph fast-moving subjects like kids, pets, or events. You can shoot in burst mode and select the best images later, reducing the pressure of timing each shot perfectly.

8. Weather Sealing and Durability

The Canon EOS R5 Mark II is built to withstand challenging conditions, with robust weather sealing that protects against dust and moisture. This makes it suitable for outdoor photographers who often shoot in unpredictable environments, such as landscapes or wildlife.

Why It's Important:

- **Reliable in Harsh Conditions**: Weather sealing ensures that your camera is protected when shooting in rain, snow, or dusty environments.
- **Professional Durability**: The camera body is made from a magnesium alloy, offering durability while keeping the camera relatively lightweight.

How Beginners Can Use It: Beginners who enjoy outdoor photography or travel will appreciate the rugged design. You can take the camera into more extreme environments without worrying as much about damage from the elements.

Conclusion

The Canon EOS R5 Mark II is packed with features that cater to both beginners and professionals. Its 45MP full-frame sensor, advanced autofocus system, 8K video capability, and in-body image stabilization make it a versatile tool for a wide range of photographic and videographic needs. Beginners can benefit from the intuitive design and helpful features like autofocus and stabilization, while professionals will appreciate the camera's high performance and flexibility.

Differences Between the R5 and R5 Mark II

The Canon EOS R5 Mark II is an upgraded version of the highly popular Canon EOS R5. Although both models share many similarities, such as a 45-megapixel full-frame sensor and high-quality video recording capabilities, the R5 Mark II introduces several enhancements that cater to both beginners and professionals. Understanding these differences is key to deciding whether the upgrade is worth it for your photography or videography needs.

In this section, we'll explore the key differences between the Canon EOS R5 and the R5 Mark II, breaking down each feature in simple terms to make it accessible for all users.

1. Improved Autofocus System

Both the R5 and R5 Mark II feature Canon's Dual Pixel CMOS autofocus system, but the Mark II takes it a step further with improved subject tracking, faster focus acquisition, and enhanced AI-driven features. The autofocus (AF) system in the R5 Mark II offers better accuracy and responsiveness, particularly in challenging situations like low-light environments or when photographing fast-moving subjects.

What's New in the R5 Mark II?

- **Enhanced AI Learning**: The R5 Mark II incorporates a more advanced AI-driven autofocus system, allowing it to better recognize and track faces, eyes, animals, and vehicles. This makes it more reliable when shooting unpredictable subjects, such as wildlife or fast-action sports.

- **Low-Light Autofocus**: The autofocus on the R5 Mark II is even more sensitive in low-light conditions, making it easier to achieve sharp focus in dark settings, such as indoor events or nighttime shoots.

Why It Matters for Beginners: For beginners, an improved autofocus system reduces the learning curve. You don't need to worry about manual focusing or losing focus on a moving subject. The camera does the heavy lifting, allowing you to focus on composition and creativity.

Why It Matters for Professionals: For professionals, the R5 Mark II's advanced AI autofocus ensures consistent and accurate tracking, even in demanding shooting environments. This is particularly useful for high-stakes shoots where missing a critical moment is not an option.

2. Faster Continuous Shooting

Both the R5 and R5 Mark II offer impressive burst shooting capabilities, which allow photographers to capture multiple frames in quick succession. However, the R5 Mark II introduces a faster shooting speed, especially with the mechanical shutter.

What's New in the R5 Mark II?

- **Higher Frame Rates**: The R5 Mark II can shoot at 30 frames per second (fps) using the electronic shutter, an increase from the 20 fps available in the original R5. With the mechanical shutter, the R5 Mark II reaches up to 15 fps, compared to 12 fps in the original R5.

Why It Matters for Beginners: For beginners experimenting with action photography—like capturing kids running, pets playing, or sports events—faster continuous shooting makes it easier to get the perfect shot. You can simply hold down the shutter button and choose the best frame afterward.

Why It Matters for Professionals: For professionals shooting fast-paced events like weddings, sports, or wildlife, the extra frames per second can be a game-changer. It increases the chances of capturing the exact moment you need, with the flexibility to choose from a larger selection of images.

3. Better Low-Light Performance

While both cameras perform well in low-light conditions, the R5 Mark II has received tweaks to improve its low-light capabilities. The sensor in the R5 Mark II is designed to handle higher ISO settings with less noise, allowing for clearer images in dark environments.

What's New in the R5 Mark II?

> **Improved ISO Performance**: The R5 Mark II maintains a higher level of detail and less grain (or noise) when shooting at high ISO levels, which are often used in low-light photography. This means that images shot in darker settings will look cleaner and sharper compared to the R5.

Why It Matters for Beginners: Beginners often struggle with low-light photography because using high ISO settings can introduce noise, which makes the photo look grainy. The improved performance of the R5 Mark II makes low-light shooting more forgiving, so beginners can shoot in dimly lit conditions without worrying as much about image quality.

Why It Matters for Professionals: For professionals, especially those working in event photography or outdoor photography during dawn or dusk, the enhanced low-light performance means you can push the camera's ISO limits further without sacrificing image quality. This allows for greater flexibility in challenging lighting conditions.

4. Enhanced Video Capabilities

Both the Canon EOS R5 and R5 Mark II are capable of 8K video recording, but the R5 Mark II introduces improvements in video performance, including better thermal management and longer recording times without overheating.

What's New in the R5 Mark II?

- **Improved Overheating Control**: One of the main criticisms of the original R5 was its tendency to overheat during extended 8K or 4K video recording sessions. The R5 Mark II features improved heat management, allowing for longer recording times without the risk of overheating.

- **Expanded Recording Options**: The R5 Mark II also offers more advanced video features, including a wider range of frame rates and improved 8K RAW recording, making it an even more attractive option for professional filmmakers.

Why It Matters for Beginners: Beginners can experiment with high-quality video recording without worrying about overheating, even during longer shoots. The expanded frame rate options also make it easier to try different creative techniques, such as slow motion.

Why It Matters for Professionals: For professional videographers, the R5 Mark II's enhanced thermal control and advanced recording options make it a more reliable tool for demanding shoots, where long recording times and high-quality footage are essential.

5. More Robust Image Stabilization

The R5 introduced in-body image stabilization (IBIS) to Canon's full-frame mirrorless lineup, providing up to 8 stops of stabilization. The R5 Mark II builds on this feature, offering more refined stabilization performance, particularly when shooting handheld or in motion.

What's New in the R5 Mark II?

> **Enhanced IBIS Performance**: The R5 Mark II improves the accuracy of its in-body image stabilization, offering smoother handheld shooting for both photos and videos. This is particularly useful for videographers who need stable footage without using a gimbal.

Why It Matters for Beginners: Beginners can take sharp handheld shots without the need for a tripod, even in low-light conditions or when using slower shutter speeds. This makes it easier to get creative and explore different shooting scenarios.

Why It Matters for Professionals: For professionals, especially those shooting handheld video or long-exposure photography, the improved IBIS allows for even greater stabilization, ensuring sharper images and smoother video footage without additional equipment.

6. User Interface and Customization Improvements

While the user interface on the R5 is already quite intuitive, the R5 Mark II introduces subtle improvements to menu navigation and customization, making the camera even easier to use.

What's New in the R5 Mark II?

- **Streamlined Menu System**: The R5 Mark II refines the layout of the menus, making it easier to navigate settings quickly, which is especially important for professionals who need to change settings on the fly.
- **Improved Button Customization**: The R5 Mark II also offers more options for button customization, allowing users to tailor the camera controls to their specific shooting style.

Why It Matters for Beginners: Beginners will find the simplified menu system easier to navigate, reducing the learning curve when accessing important features. The ability to customize buttons also allows beginners to streamline their workflow as they become more comfortable with the camera.

Why It Matters for Professionals: For professionals, the increased customization options can significantly enhance workflow efficiency, enabling quick access to frequently used settings and functions during high-pressure shoots.

7. Battery Life Enhancements

Battery life is always a concern for photographers and videographers, especially during long shoots or events. While both the R5 and R5 Mark II use the same battery type (LP-E6NH), the R5 Mark II offers slightly improved battery efficiency, allowing for longer shooting sessions.

What's New in the R5 Mark II?

> **Better Power Management**: The R5 Mark II has improved power management, meaning you can shoot for longer on a single battery charge compared to the original R5.

Why It Matters for Beginners: For beginners who might not have a lot of spare batteries, improved battery life means you can shoot longer without interruption, making it easier to focus on learning and experimenting with different features.

Why It Matters for Professionals: For professionals, longer battery life means fewer interruptions during important shoots, such as weddings or events, where missing a moment could be critical

Conclusion

The Canon EOS R5 Mark II builds on the success of the original R5 by introducing several meaningful improvements in areas like autofocus, video performance, continuous shooting speed, low-light capability, and user interface. While both cameras are excellent tools for photographers and videographers, the R5 Mark II offers a more refined experience that caters to both beginners and professionals. Whether you're just starting out or looking to upgrade your gear, understanding these key differences will help you decide which model is right for you.

Who is this Camera For? (Beginners vs. Professionals)

The Canon EOS R5 Mark II is a versatile camera that caters to both beginners and professionals, offering features that can meet the demands of those just starting out in photography as well as seasoned experts. Understanding who this camera is best suited for requires a breakdown of its key functionalities and how these can benefit different users at various skill levels.

In this section, we will explore why the Canon EOS R5 Mark II is an excellent option for both beginner photographers and professionals. We'll discuss its ease of use, advanced features, and how it accommodates a wide range of photography needs.

1. Canon EOS R5 Mark II for Beginners

For beginners, choosing the right camera can feel overwhelming due to the technical jargon and variety of options available. The Canon EOS R5 Mark II simplifies this decision by offering features that make photography more accessible while still providing room for growth as skills improve.

Ease of Use for Beginners

Intuitive Interface and Customizable Menus

The Canon EOS R5 Mark II features a user-friendly interface, making it easy for beginners to navigate through settings and functions. The menus are logically arranged, and beginners can customize the layout to prioritize the tools they use most frequently. This customization reduces the learning curve, allowing newcomers to focus on the basics without getting lost in the camera's more complex features.

Automatic and Scene Modes

The R5 Mark II includes automatic shooting modes and scene modes that allow beginners to take great photos without needing to understand manual settings. These modes adjust the camera's settings automatically to suit the shooting environment, whether you're photographing landscapes, portraits, or action shots.

- **Auto Mode**: In Auto Mode, the camera chooses the optimal settings for you, which is perfect for those just starting out. You can point and shoot without worrying about technicalities like ISO, aperture, and shutter speed.
- **Scene Modes**: Scene Modes are designed to capture specific types of photos, such as portraits, landscapes, or sports. This helps beginners take better pictures in different situations without needing to adjust many settings manually.

Learning the Basics with Confidence

Helpful On-Screen Guides

The R5 Mark II also provides on-screen explanations and tips for certain features and settings. Beginners can use this built-in guidance to better understand how the camera works without having to consult a manual constantly. This feature encourages learning while shooting, allowing users to develop their skills over time.

Reliable Autofocus System

One of the biggest challenges for new photographers is mastering focus. The R5 Mark II's advanced autofocus system takes the guesswork out of focusing, automatically locking onto subjects—whether they're stationary or moving. The camera's ability to track faces, eyes, and animals makes it much easier for beginners to capture sharp images consistently.

In-Body Image Stabilization (IBIS)

Beginners often struggle with camera shake, which can result in blurry photos. The R5 Mark II's in-body image stabilization helps reduce this issue, providing up to 8 stops of stabilization. This feature ensures sharper images even when shooting handheld, giving new photographers more confidence in their shots.

Room to Grow

Manual Mode and Advanced Settings

While the R5 Mark II offers a variety of automatic settings, it also provides manual controls that allow beginners to experiment with more advanced photography techniques as they grow in confidence. Users can switch to Manual Mode and start learning how to control exposure settings such as ISO, aperture, and shutter speed.

High-Quality Sensor for Learning

The 45-megapixel full-frame sensor is one of the R5 Mark II's standout features. Even as a beginner, you'll benefit from the high-quality images this camera can produce. This means you won't quickly outgrow the camera's capabilities. As you progress, the quality of the images will still be more than sufficient, allowing room for growth without needing an upgrade.

Conclusion for Beginners

The Canon EOS R5 Mark II is ideal for beginners because it offers easy-to-use features like Auto and Scene Modes, reliable autofocus, and in-body image stabilization. At the same time, it provides room to grow with more advanced settings as the user becomes more experienced. Beginners will appreciate the intuitive interface, built-in guides, and the ability to produce professional-quality images from the start.

2. Canon EOS R5 Mark II for Professionals

For professionals, the Canon EOS R5 Mark II offers cutting-edge features and performance capabilities that meet the demands of high-level photography and videography. From its robust sensor to advanced video options, the R5 Mark II delivers on the precision and flexibility that professionals require.

Professional-Grade Image Quality

45-Megapixel Full-Frame Sensor

The high-resolution 45-megapixel sensor is perfect for professionals who need large image files for commercial or editorial work. This sensor provides incredible detail and dynamic range, allowing for stunning images in a variety of shooting conditions. The sensor is also excellent for producing large prints or cropping images without sacrificing quality.

RAW Image Capture

Professionals often prefer to shoot in RAW format, which allows for greater flexibility in post-processing. The R5 Mark II offers robust RAW shooting capabilities, including Dual Pixel RAW, which provides even more control over focus and bokeh in post-production. This level of flexibility is essential for professionals who need the utmost control over their final images.

Advanced Autofocus and Customization

AI-Powered Autofocus System

For professionals, precision and speed are key. The R5 Mark II features an advanced AI-driven autofocus system that excels in tracking moving subjects, such as athletes, wildlife, or models in fast-paced environments. The camera's ability to recognize faces, eyes, animals, and even vehicles ensures that professionals can capture critical moments with precision.

Customizable Controls

Professionals often need to change settings quickly on the go. The R5 Mark II allows for extensive customization of buttons and dials, enabling users to set up the camera in a way that best suits their shooting style. This level of customization can significantly improve workflow efficiency, especially in fast-paced or high-pressure environments.

Video Capabilities for Professionals

8K and 4K Video Recording

The R5 Mark II is an excellent tool for professional videographers. It offers 8K video recording at up to 30 frames per second (fps), providing unparalleled detail for high-end productions. It also supports 4K at up to 120 fps, perfect for capturing slow-motion footage. This flexibility makes the R5 Mark II a great choice for videographers working on commercials, documentaries, or cinematic projects.

Improved Thermal Management

A key improvement in the R5 Mark II is its better thermal management system, which allows for longer video recording times without the risk of overheating. This is critical for professionals who need to shoot extended video sessions without interruption.

High-Speed Performance

Faster Continuous Shooting

For professionals working in fields such as sports, wildlife, or event photography, the R5 Mark II's faster continuous shooting speeds are invaluable. With the electronic shutter, the camera can shoot at up to 30 fps, ensuring that no critical moment is missed. The mechanical shutter offers up to 15 fps, providing fast and accurate performance even when capturing high-speed action.

Dual Card Slots

The R5 Mark II includes dual card slots, one for CFexpress cards and another for SD cards. This is important for professionals who need redundancy when shooting important events, as it allows for simultaneous recording to both cards. It also provides the option to separate different types of files, such as saving RAW files to one card and JPEGs to the other.

Robust Build and Durability

Weather Sealing

The Canon EOS R5 Mark II is built to withstand harsh conditions, making it ideal for professionals who often work in challenging environments. Its durable, weather-sealed body can handle rain, dust, and other environmental factors, ensuring reliable performance even in extreme conditions.

Long Battery Life

For professionals who spend long hours shooting, battery life is a crucial consideration. The R5 Mark II has improved power management, allowing for longer battery life compared to its predecessor. This reduces downtime on set or in the field, enabling more time to focus on capturing the perfect shot.

Conclusion for Professionals

The Canon EOS R5 Mark II is packed with features that cater to the needs of professionals, including its 45-megapixel sensor, advanced autofocus system, and robust video capabilities. Whether shooting high-resolution stills, fast-paced action, or 8K video, the R5 Mark II delivers the performance and reliability that professionals demand. The camera's extensive customization options, high-speed shooting, and durable build make it a versatile tool for a wide range of professional applications.

Conclusion: A Camera for All

The Canon EOS R5 Mark II is designed to be a camera that appeals to both beginners and professionals. Its ease of use, intuitive controls, and built-in guidance make it perfect for those just starting out, while its advanced features, high-resolution sensor, and professional-grade video capabilities make it a powerful tool for experts. Whether you're looking to capture family memories or work on a high-stakes commercial shoot, the Canon EOS R5 Mark II offers the flexibility, performance, and quality to suit photographers and videographers at every skill level.

CHAPTER 2

GETTING STARTED WITH THE R5 MARK II

Unboxing and Setting Up the Camera

When you first get your hands on the Canon EOS R5 Mark II, it's important to start on the right foot by carefully unboxing and setting up the camera. Whether you're a beginner eager to take your first professional-quality shots or a seasoned photographer looking to familiarize yourself with the latest gear, the setup process is straightforward. In this section, we will walk you through the unboxing experience and explain each component while offering clear, simple instructions on how to properly set up your new camera for the first time.

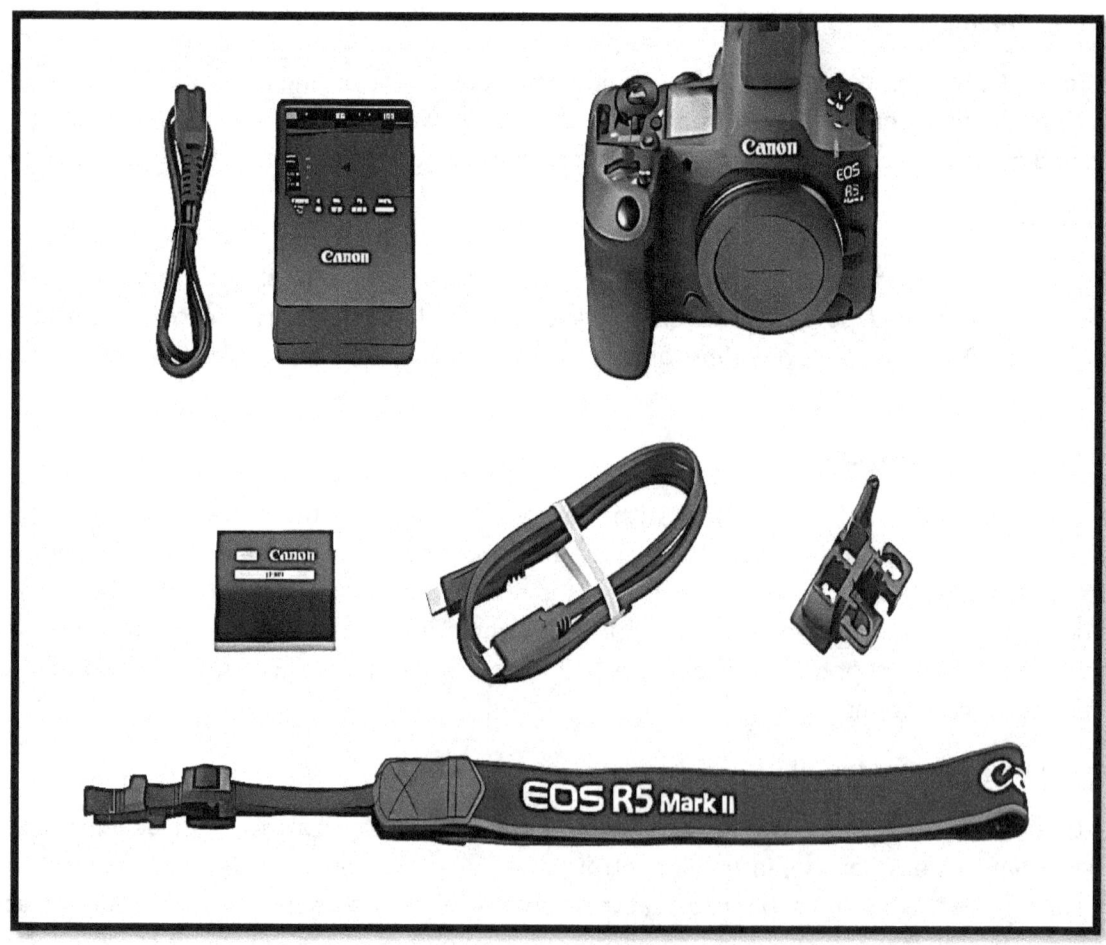

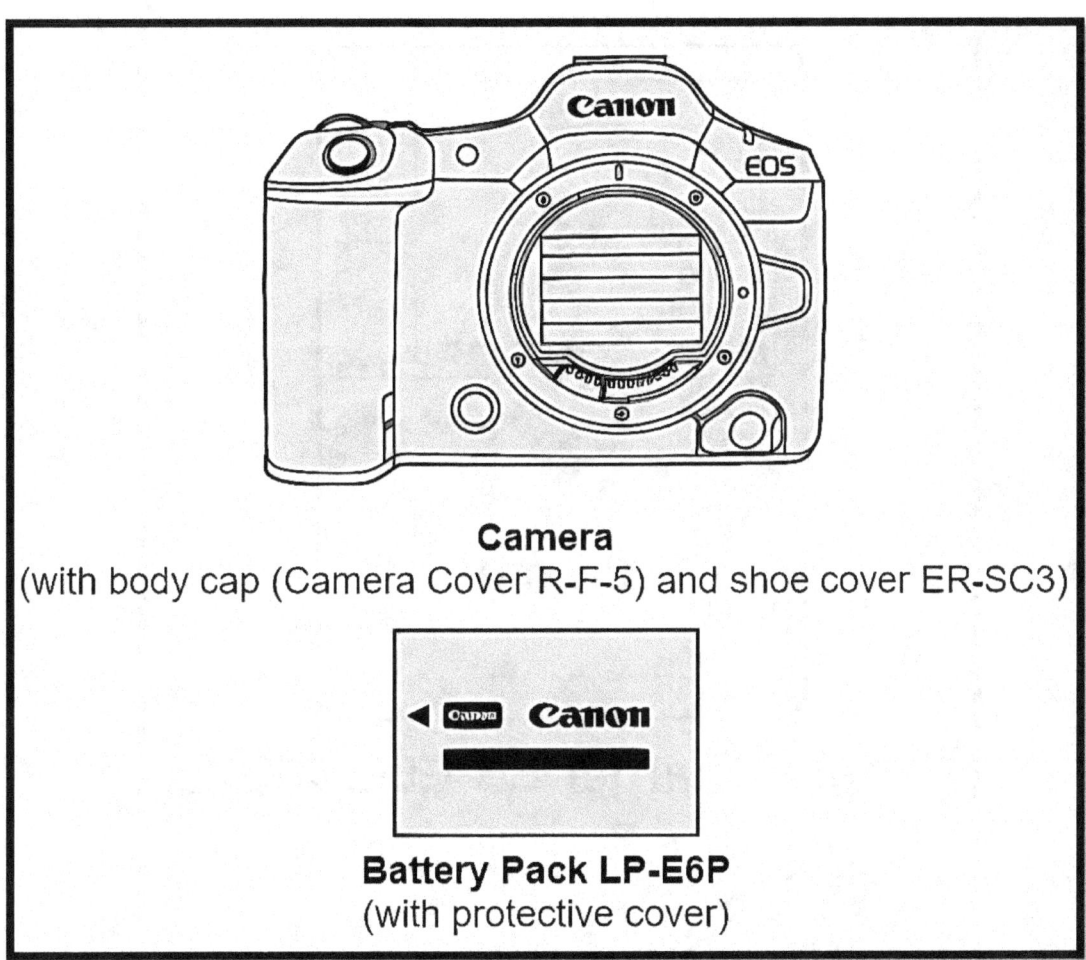

Camera
(with body cap (Camera Cover R-F-5) and shoe cover ER-SC3)

Battery Pack LP-E6P
(with protective cover)

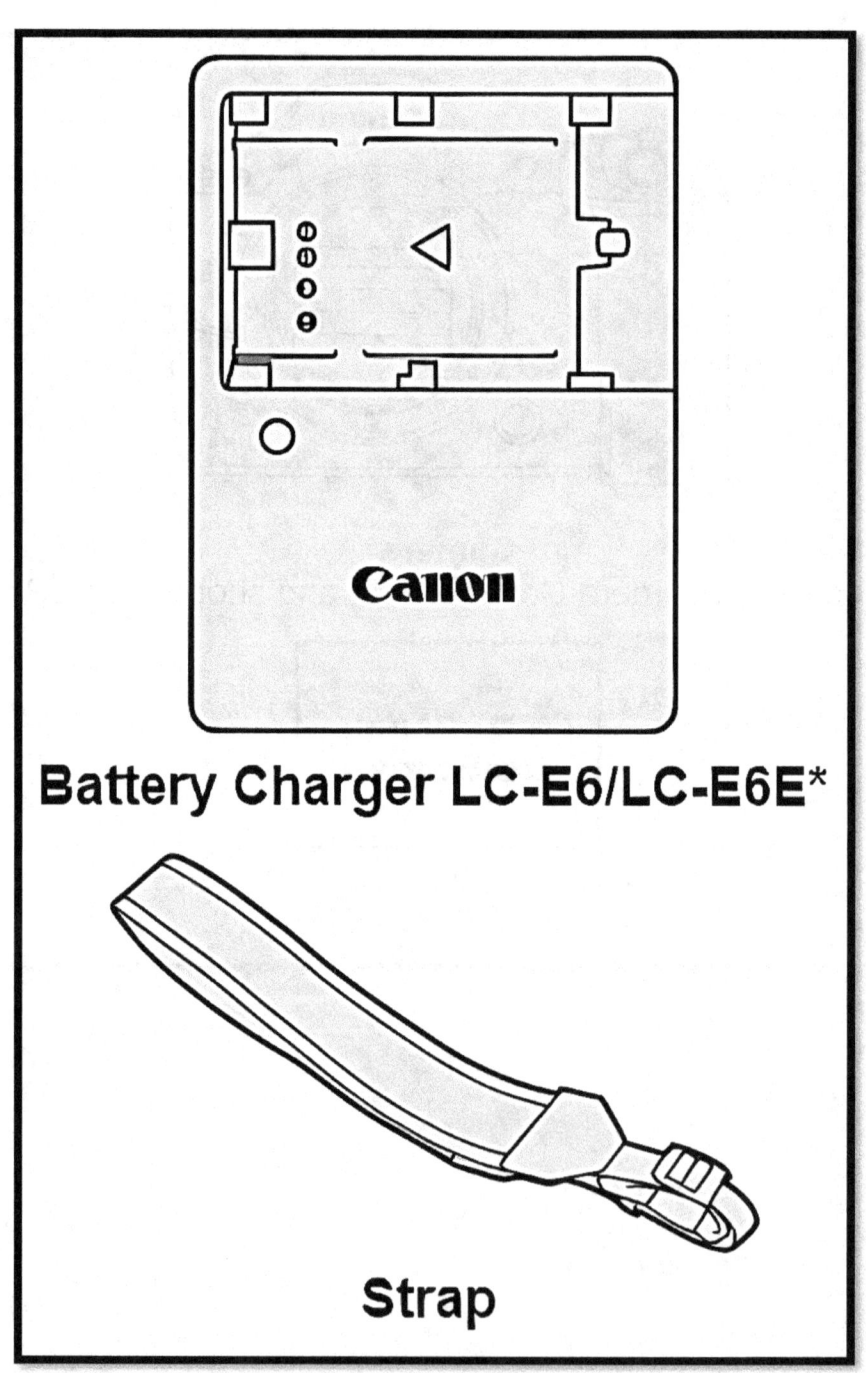

Battery Charger LC-E6/LC-E6E*

Strap

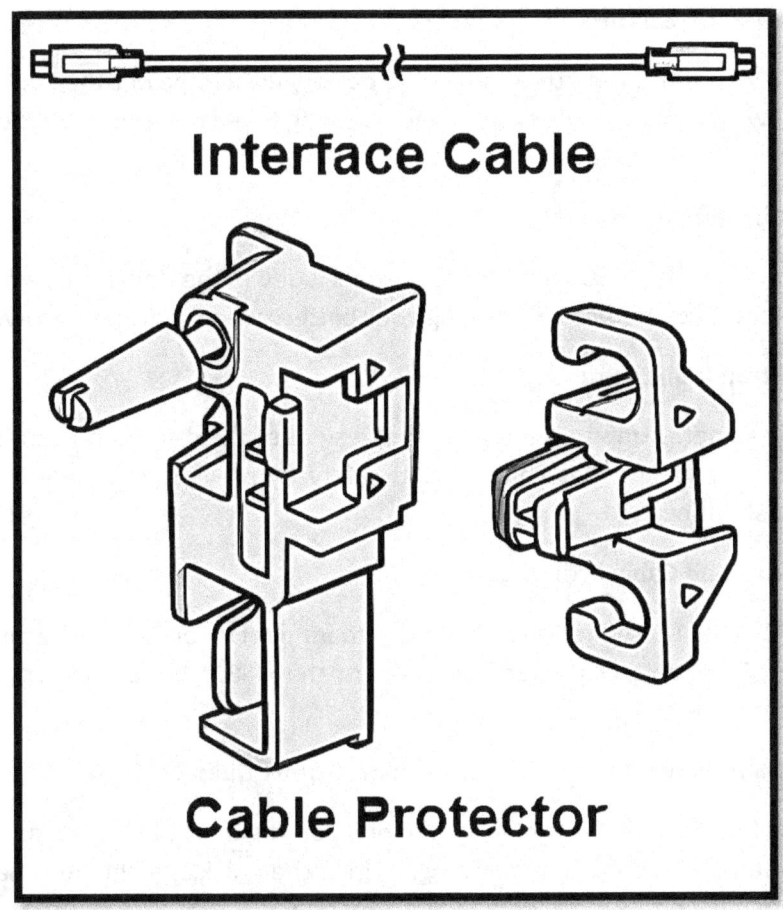

1. Unboxing the Canon EOS R5 Mark II

When you open the box containing your new Canon EOS R5 Mark II, you'll notice several components neatly packed inside. Here's what you should expect to find and a brief explanation of each item:

What's in the Box:

- **Canon EOS R5 Mark II Camera Body**

    This is the main component of the camera. The camera body houses the sensor, buttons, ports, and controls you will use to take photos and videos.

- **RF Lens (Optional, depending on kit)**

    If you purchased the camera as part of a kit, it might come with an RF lens, which is compatible with Canon's new mirrorless RF mount system. This lens is what allows you to focus light onto the camera sensor.

- **Battery Pack (LP-E6NH)**

  The LP-E6NH is the standard rechargeable battery used to power the Canon EOS R5 Mark II. This powerful battery offers extended shooting time, ensuring that your camera stays powered for longer periods.

- **Battery Charger (LC-E6)**

  The charger for the LP-E6NH battery is also included in the box. It's essential for keeping your camera ready for use by charging your battery when it's running low.

- **Camera Strap (Canon Branded)**

  This is the camera strap that attaches to the sides of the camera body. It's branded with Canon's logo and provides comfort and safety by preventing accidental drops during handheld shooting.

- **USB-C Cable and Cable Protector**

  The USB-C cable is used for charging the camera directly or for transferring data to your computer. The cable protector helps secure the USB cable to prevent damage while shooting tethered.

- **Canon EOS R5 Mark II User Manual and Quick Start Guide**

  You'll also find a printed user manual and quick start guide to help you familiarize yourself with the camera's controls and settings. While the quick start guide is handy for setup, the user manual offers more detailed information.

- **Lens Cap and Body Cap**

  These caps are essential for protecting the camera's sensor and lens when they are not in use. The body cap protects the camera's sensor from dust and debris when a lens is not attached, while the lens cap shields the front element of the lens.

2. Setting Up the Camera for the First Time

Now that you've unboxed your Canon EOS R5 Mark II, it's time to set up the camera and get it ready for shooting. In this section, we'll guide you through the steps involved in setting up the camera, starting from installing the battery and lens to powering it on and configuring initial settings.

Step 1: Installing the Battery

Before you can start using your camera, you need to install the battery. Follow these simple steps:

- **Locate the Battery Compartment**

    The battery compartment is found at the bottom of the camera. Slide the latch to open the battery door.

- **Insert the Battery (LP-E6NH)**

    Take the LP-E6NH battery and align it with the contacts in the battery compartment. Ensure that the Canon logo is facing out and gently slide the battery into place. Once it clicks, you know it's secure.

- **Close the Battery Compartment**

    Once the battery is inside, close the compartment door and make sure it clicks shut.

- **Charge the Battery**

    If the battery is not fully charged, it's a good idea to plug it into the charger before using the camera extensively. Simply remove the battery, place it in the charger (LC-E6), and connect the charger to a power outlet. The LED light on the charger will indicate the charging status. Green means fully charged, while orange means it's still charging.

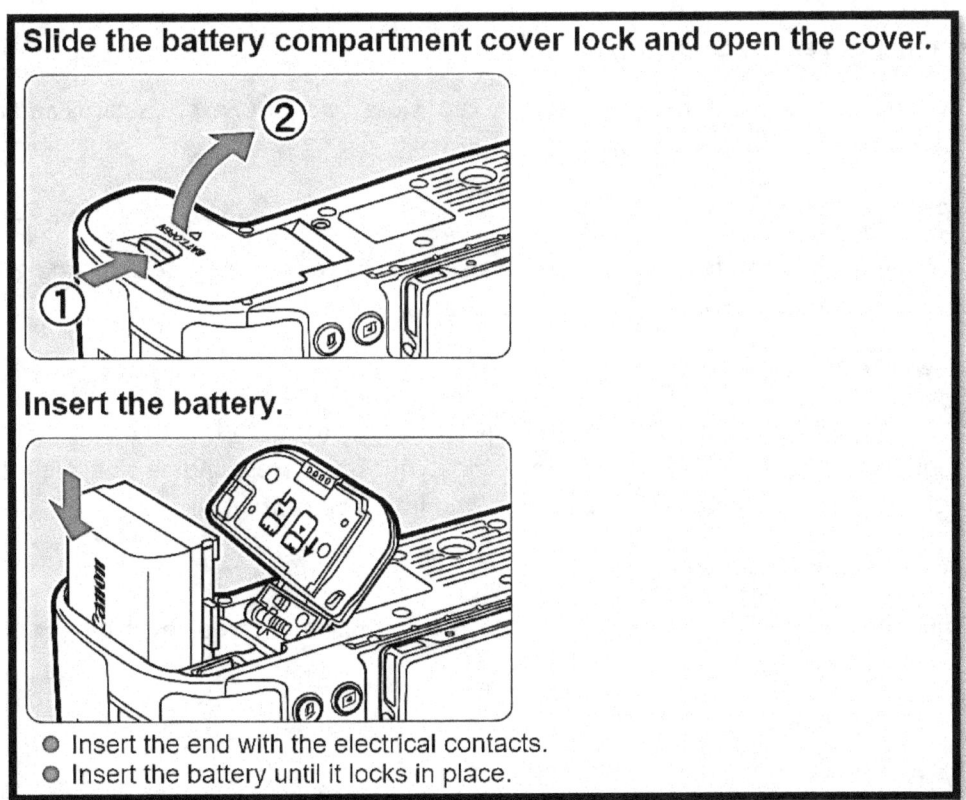

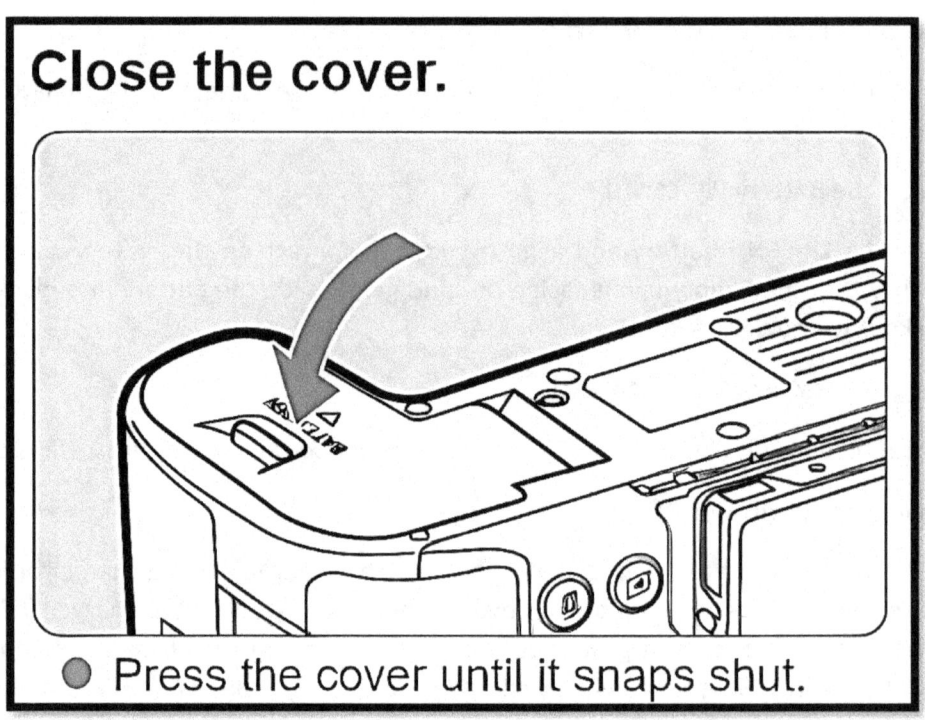

Step 2: Inserting a Memory Card

The Canon EOS R5 Mark II features dual memory card slots: one for CFexpress cards and another for SD cards. Here's how to insert your memory card:

- **Open the Memory Card Slot Door**

    The memory card slots are located on the side of the camera, next to the hand grip. Slide the compartment door open to access the slots.

- **Insert the Memory Card**

    You can insert either a CFexpress card or an SD card (or both for redundancy). If you're using a CFexpress card, make sure to insert it into the corresponding slot. Align the card with the arrow on the card and gently push it into place until it clicks.

- **Close the Compartment**

    Once the card is securely inserted, close the compartment door by sliding it back into place until it locks.

Slide the cover to open it.

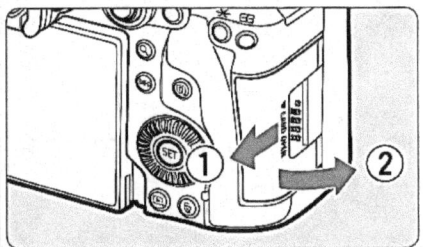

- Pull the card slot cover toward you to open it.

Insert the card.

Card 1 (CFexpress card)   Card 2 (SD card)

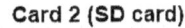

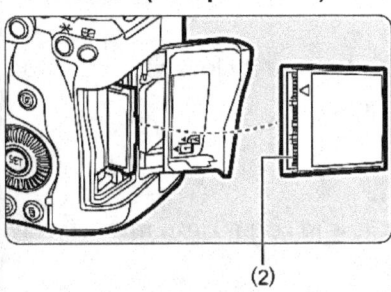 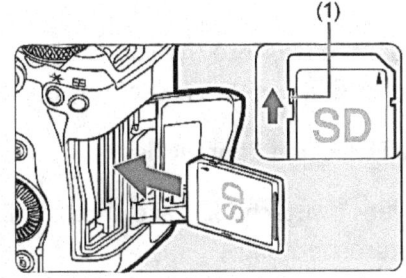

- The card in the rear card slot is [1] (CFexpress card), and the one in front of it is [2] (SD card).
- CFexpress card: With the card label facing you, insert the open side of the card (2) into the card slot. **Inserting cards the wrong way may damage the camera.**
- The gray card-eject button pops out.
- SD card: With the card label facing you, insert the card into the card slot until it clicks into place.

Close the cover.

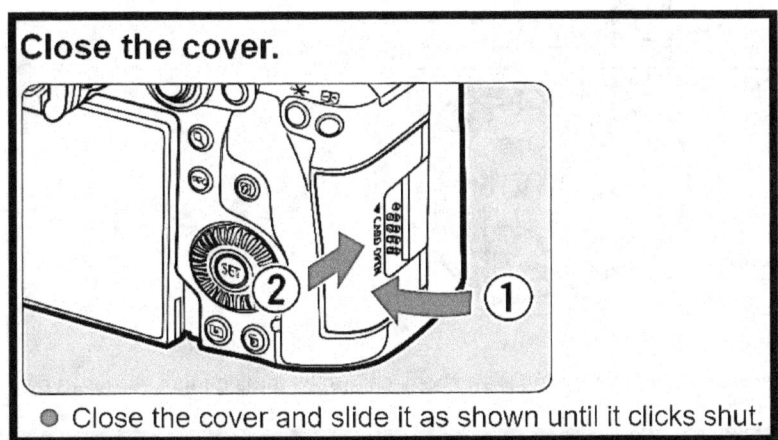

- Close the cover and slide it as shown until it clicks shut.

Step 3: Attaching the Lens

If you have an RF lens or any compatible lens, the next step is to attach it to the camera body.

- **Remove the Body Cap and Lens Cap**

    Start by removing the body cap from the camera and the rear cap from the lens. This will expose the camera's sensor and the lens's mounting ring.

- **Align the Mounting Marks**

    Look for the red dot on the lens and the red dot on the camera's lens mount. Align these two dots.

- **Attach the Len**

    Gently press the lens into the camera body and rotate it clockwise until you hear a click. This indicates that the lens is securely attached.

- **Check the Focus and Zoom Rings**

    Once the lens is attached, make sure the focus and zoom rings move freely. You're now ready to start shooting!

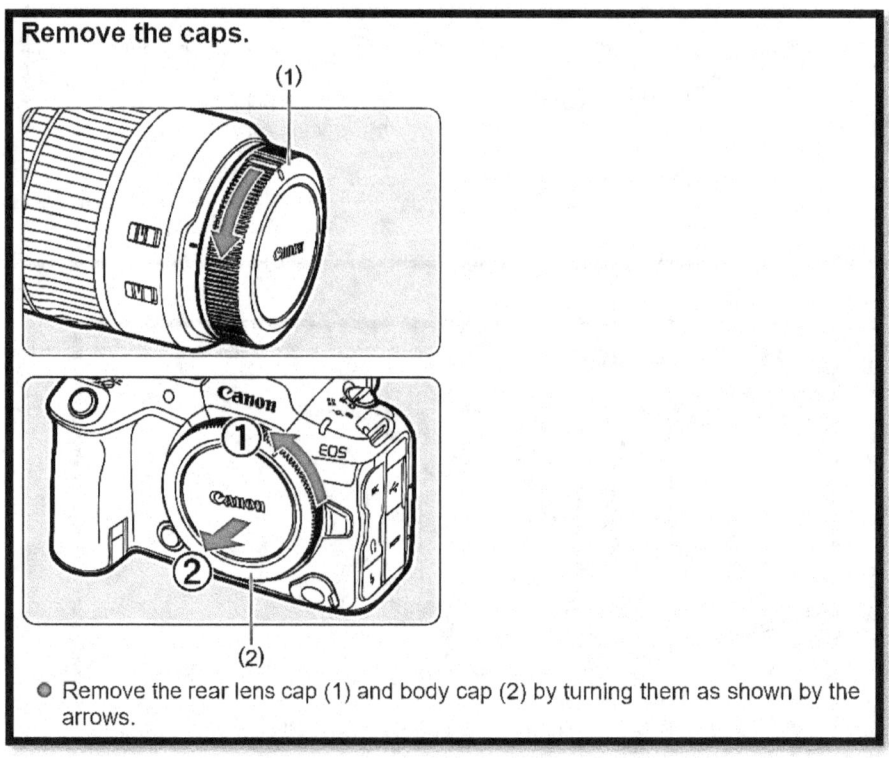

22

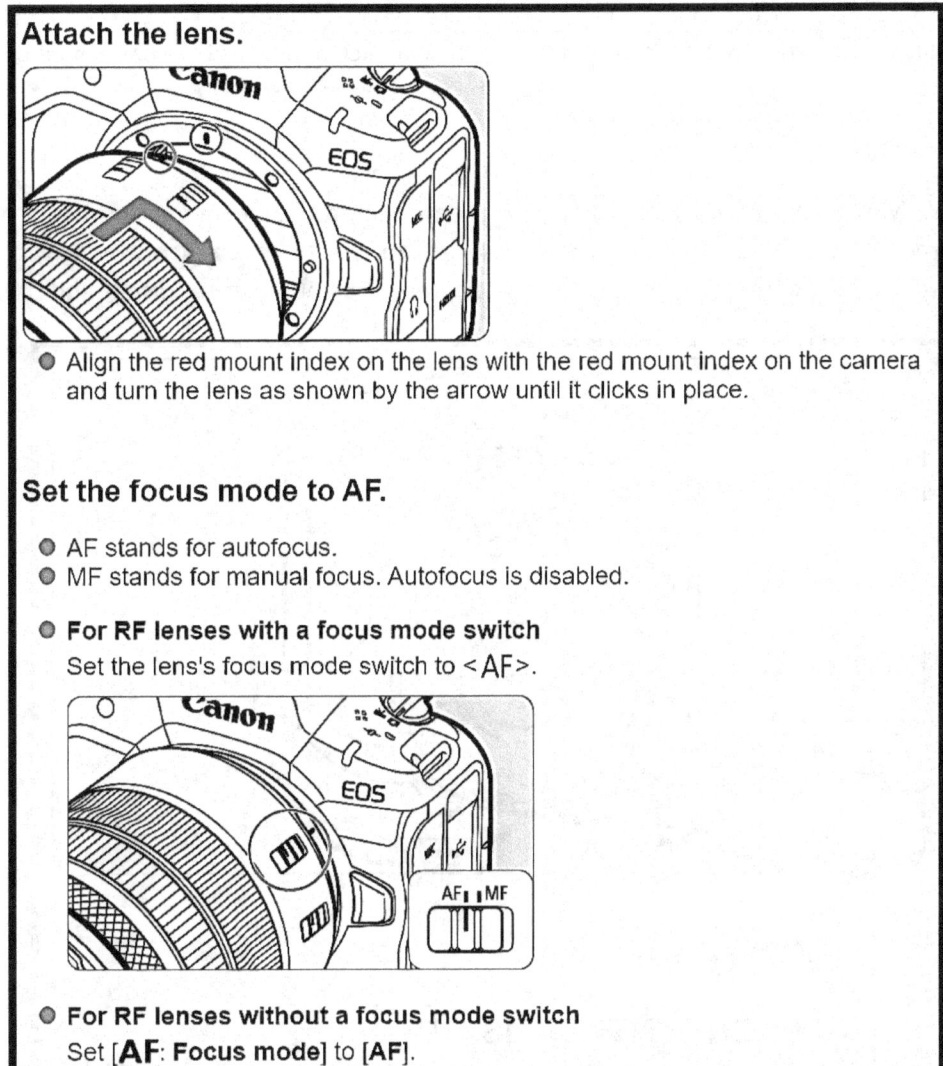

Step 4: Powering On the Camera

With the battery and memory card installed and the lens attached, it's time to power on your Canon EOS R5 Mark II.

- **Locate the Power Switch**

    The power switch is located on the top of the camera, near the mode dial. It is a small switch that you'll need to flick to the "ON" position.

- **Initial Setup Screen**

The first time you turn on the camera, you will be prompted to select your preferred language, time zone, and date format. Use the touchscreen or the directional buttons to make your selections and confirm them by pressing the "Set" button.

- **Format the Memory Card**

    It's always a good idea to format your memory card the first time you use it in a new camera. Go to the "Menu" button, navigate to the "Wrench" icon (which represents settings), and choose "Format Card." Select the card you want to format and press "OK."

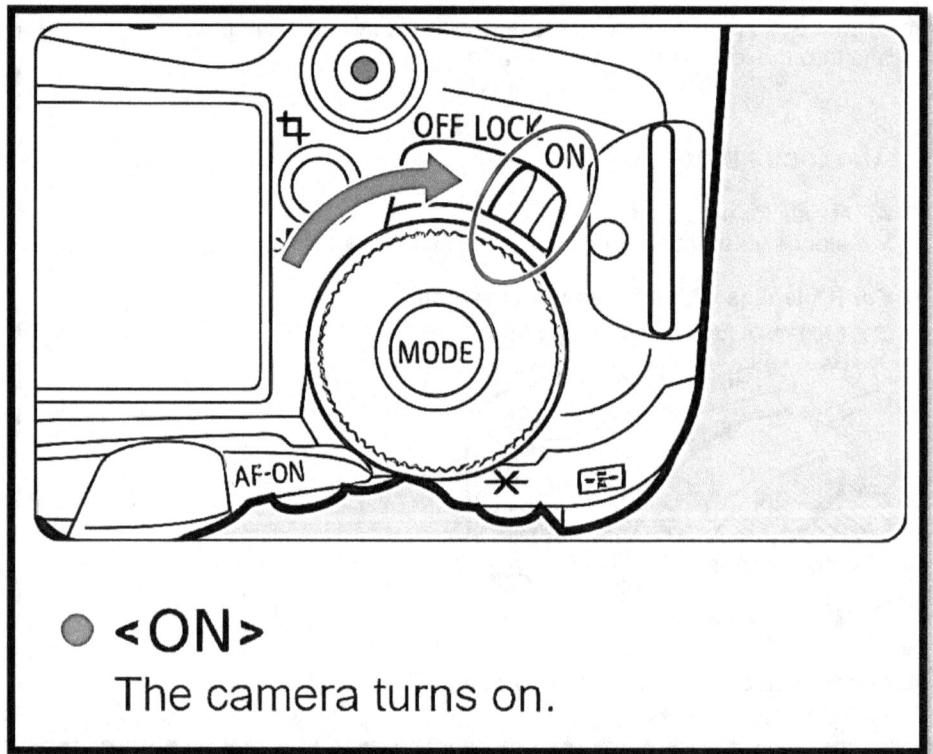

3. Basic Settings for First-Time Use

Once your camera is powered on, there are a few basic settings you should adjust before you start shooting. These settings will help you get the best performance out of your Canon EOS R5 Mark II from the start.

Adjusting the Image Quality Setting

By default, the Canon EOS R5 Mark II may be set to capture images in JPEG format. However, you might want to shoot in RAW for higher image quality, especially if you plan to do post-processing.

- **Go to the Menu**

Press the "Menu" button and navigate to the "Image Quality" settings.

- **Select RAW or JPEG**

    You can choose to shoot in RAW, JPEG, or both. RAW files retain more data, allowing for better post-processing, while JPEGs are smaller and easier to share directly.

- **Confirm Your Selection**

    Once you've selected your preferred image quality, press "OK."

Setting the Autofocus Mode

The R5 Mark II has several autofocus modes depending on your shooting needs.

- **Go to the Autofocus Menu**

    Press the "Menu" button and navigate to the autofocus settings.

- **Choose Your AF Mode**

    Beginners might prefer "One-Shot AF" for stationary subjects, while professionals might use "AI Servo AF" for moving subjects.

- **Confirm Your Selection**

    After choosing the AF mode, press "Set" to save your choice.

Checking ISO Settings

ISO determines how sensitive your camera sensor is to light.

- **Use Auto ISO**

    For beginners, Auto ISO is a great option as the camera will automatically adjust ISO based on lighting conditions.

- **For Professionals**

    You can manually set ISO depending on your needs. Lower ISO is ideal for bright conditions, while higher ISO is useful for low light, though it introduces more noise.

Conclusion

Setting up the Canon EOS R5 Mark II is a straightforward process, whether you're a beginner or a seasoned professional. From unboxing the camera and installing the battery to attaching the lens and adjusting key settings, these steps ensure that your camera is ready to deliver its best performance. Whether you're shooting your first photo or preparing for a professional shoot, these foundational setup steps will help you make the most out of your new Canon EOS R5 Mark II.

Basic Menu Navigation and Customization

When you first begin using the Canon EOS R5 Mark II, one of the most important skills to learn is how to navigate and customize the camera's menu system. Whether you're a beginner photographer or an experienced professional, understanding how to efficiently move through the menus and set them up to suit your specific shooting style can significantly enhance your experience with the camera. In this section, we'll break down the basic structure of the Canon EOS R5 Mark II's menu system and walk you through the customization options available.

1. Overview of the Canon EOS R5 Mark II Menu System

The Canon EOS R5 Mark II has a well-organized and comprehensive menu system that allows you to control everything from image quality and autofocus settings to custom button assignments and display preferences. The menu is divided into several main categories, making it easy to navigate and find the settings you need.

Menu Layout:

- **Shooting (Red)**

    These settings control everything related to image capture, such as picture quality, autofocus modes, and exposure settings.

- **Playback (Blue)**

    This section allows you to review your images and videos, delete them, or view shooting information.

- **Network (Green)**

    If you're using the camera's wireless features, such as Wi-Fi or Bluetooth, this menu helps you manage connections and sharing settings.

- **Setup (Yellow)**

    The setup menu controls the camera's basic functions, such as display brightness, date and time, and file numbering.

- **Custom Functions (Orange)**

    This is where you can dive into advanced customization, like assigning specific functions to buttons or creating custom shooting modes.

- **My Menu (Green Tab with a Star)**

A fully customizable menu where you can add frequently used settings for quick access.

2. Navigating the Menu System

Navigating the Canon EOS R5 Mark II's menu is simple, but it's essential to understand how to move through it efficiently. The camera provides two main ways to navigate the menu: through the touchscreen interface or using the physical controls (buttons and dials).

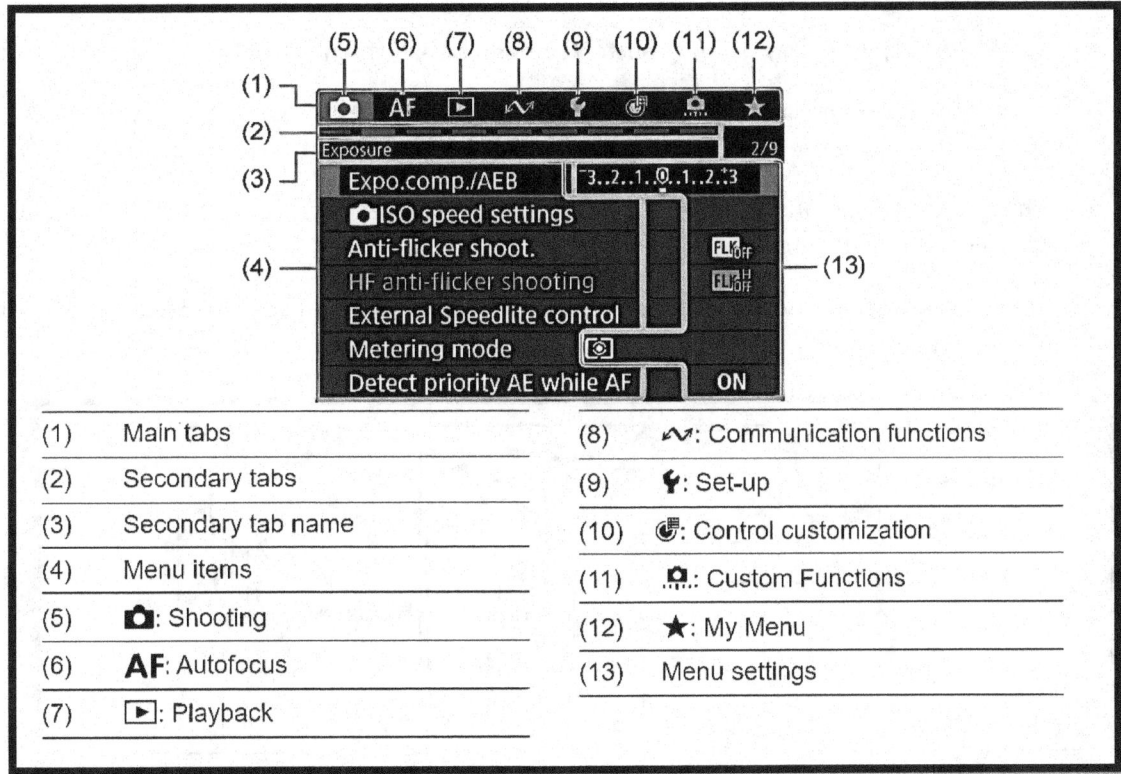

Using the Touchscreen:

The Canon EOS R5 Mark II comes with a responsive, high-resolution touchscreen that makes menu navigation very intuitive. Here's how to use it:

- **Swipe and Tap**: Just like a smartphone, you can swipe through different menu pages and tap on the settings you want to adjust.

- **Scroll**: For long menu lists, simply scroll up or down with your finger to find the option you need.

- **Quick Access Menu**: Swiping down from the top of the screen brings up a quick access menu, where you can adjust common settings like ISO, exposure compensation, and white balance without diving deep into the main menu.

Using Physical Buttons and Dials:

If you prefer a more tactile approach, you can navigate the menu using the physical buttons and dials on the camera. Here's how:

- **Menu Button**: Press the "Menu" button to open or exit the main menu.

- **Multi-Controller (Joystick)**: This small joystick is located on the back of the camera. You can use it to move the selection up, down, left, or right through the menu options.

- **Main Dial**: Located on top of the camera near the shutter button, the main dial can also be used to scroll through settings.

- **Set Button**: Once you've highlighted the option you want to adjust, press the "Set" button in the middle of the multi-controller to select or confirm your choice.

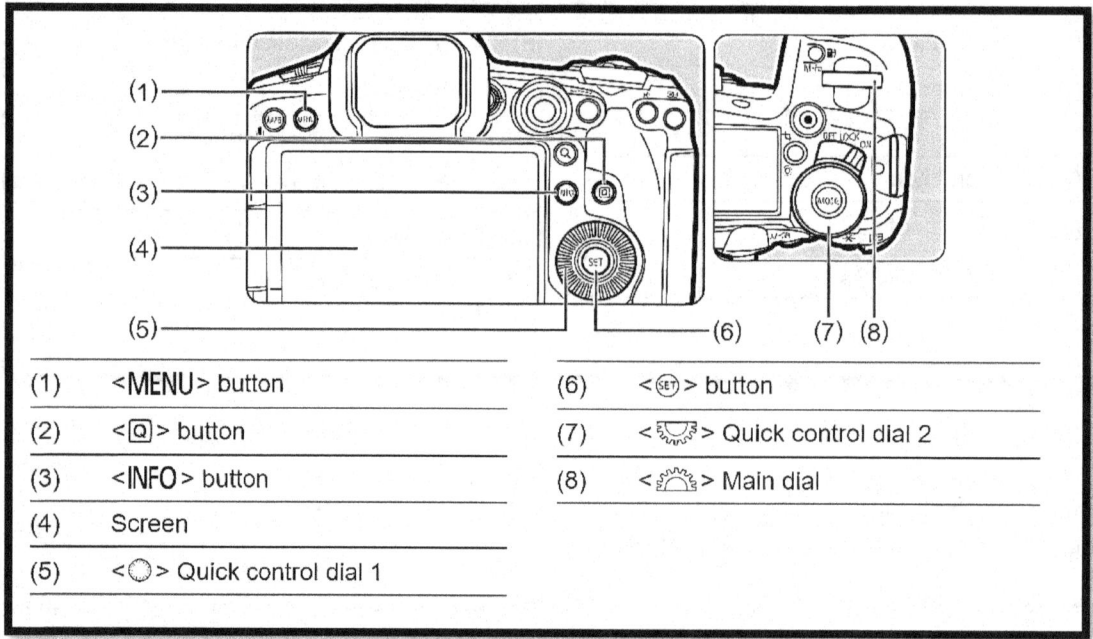

(1)	\<MENU\> button
(2)	\<Q\> button
(3)	\<INFO\> button
(4)	Screen
(5)	\<○\> Quick control dial 1

(6)	\<SET\> button
(7)	\<🔘\> Quick control dial 2
(8)	\<🔘\> Main dial

3. Important Menu Settings for Beginners

If you're new to the Canon EOS R5 Mark II, there are a few essential menu settings you'll want to familiarize yourself with first. These basic settings will help you get started and make sure your camera is configured to capture high-quality images.

a) Image Quality

Menu Path: [Shooting Menu] → [Image Quality]

The Canon EOS R5 Mark II allows you to shoot in both RAW and JPEG formats, or a combination of the two. For beginners, starting with JPEG is often simpler, as these files are easier to manage and share. However, if you want the best image quality and flexibility in post-processing, RAW is the way to go. RAW files contain more data, allowing for greater editing possibilities.

- **RAW**: Best for professionals who plan to edit photos extensively.
- **JPEG**: Ideal for beginners or when you need smaller files.
- **RAW + JPEG**: Offers the best of both worlds, saving both a high-quality RAW file and a ready-to-share JPEG.

b) Autofocus Mode

Menu Path: [Shooting Menu] → [AF Method]

The Canon EOS R5 Mark II has advanced autofocus (AF) capabilities. Beginners may want to start with a more basic AF mode, like "One Shot," while professionals may prefer the flexibility of "Servo AF" for tracking moving subjects.

- **One-Shot AF**: Best for still subjects like portraits or landscapes.
- **Servo AF**: Ideal for moving subjects, such as wildlife or sports photography.

c) ISO Settings

Menu Path: [Shooting Menu] → [ISO Speed Settings]

ISO controls the camera's sensitivity to light. For most beginners, leaving ISO in "Auto" is a good choice, as the camera will automatically adjust the ISO based on the lighting conditions. Professionals might want more control and will likely adjust ISO manually to achieve specific results.

- **Auto ISO**: Great for most general photography situations.
- **Manual ISO**: Best for professional use, especially in tricky lighting conditions.

4. Advanced Menu Customization for Professionals

While beginners can get by with the default settings, professionals will likely want to customize the Canon EOS R5 Mark II's menu to suit their particular shooting style. The camera offers numerous customization options, allowing you to streamline your workflow and make quick adjustments on the fly.

a) Customizing the Quick Control Screen

Menu Path: [Setup Menu] → [Custom Functions] → [Customize Quick Control]

The Quick Control screen is a customizable interface that lets you access your most-used settings with just a few taps. By default, it includes settings like ISO, white balance, and autofocus modes, but you can modify it to include other settings that you frequently adjust, such as picture profiles or frame rates for video.

> **Add/Remove Settings**: You can easily add or remove settings from the Quick Control screen by navigating to the customization menu and selecting the ones you want to display.

b) Custom Buttons

Menu Path: [Custom Functions] → [Customize Buttons]

For professionals, speed and efficiency are critical during shoots, so the Canon EOS R5 Mark II allows you to assign specific functions to various buttons on the camera. For example, you can assign one button to switch between autofocus modes, while another might activate eye-detection AF.

- **AF-ON Button**: You can customize this button to handle back-button focus, a popular feature among professional photographers who want to separate focusing from the shutter button.
- **Multi-Function (M-Fn) Button**: You can assign this button to quickly access settings like ISO or white balance.

c) Custom Shooting Modes (C1, C2, C3)

Menu Path: [Shooting Menu] → [Custom Shooting Mode (C1-C3)]

The Canon EOS R5 Mark II allows you to save up to three custom shooting modes, which is particularly helpful for professionals who frequently switch between different types of photography. For instance, you can save one mode for landscape photography, another for portrait sessions, and a third for action shots.

- **Save Settings**: After configuring your preferred settings, navigate to the Custom Shooting Mode menu and select "Register." Choose one of the available slots (C1, C2, or C3) to save your configuration.
- **Recalling Custom Modes**: When you need to switch to a custom mode, simply turn the mode dial to C1, C2, or C3, and all your saved settings will be applied.

5. Using the "My Menu" for Quick Access

The Canon EOS R5 Mark II has a "My Menu" feature, which allows you to create a personalized menu containing your most frequently accessed settings. This is particularly useful for both beginners and professionals who want to avoid constantly diving into the main menu to make adjustments.

Setting Up "My Menu":

1. **Go to "My Menu"**

   Press the "Menu" button and scroll to the green tab with the star icon. This is the "My Menu" section.

2. **Add Items**

   Select "Add My Menu Tab" and choose the settings you want to add to your custom menu. You can include anything from image quality settings to autofocus options or even network settings.

3. **Rearrange or Delete Items**

   Once you've added items, you can rearrange them by selecting "Sort" or delete items you no longer need by selecting "Delete Item."

4. **Access "My Menu" Quickly**

   Once set up, you can access "My Menu" with just one press of the "Menu" button, allowing for rapid adjustments without navigating through multiple tabs.

Conclusion

Understanding the Canon EOS R5 Mark II's menu system and customizing it to suit your specific needs is essential for both beginners and professionals. The menu is thoughtfully organized into categories that allow for easy navigation, while the ability to customize buttons, the Quick Control screen, and "My Menu" makes the camera adaptable to different shooting styles. Whether you're just starting out or have years of experience, taking the time to configure the menu system can greatly improve your efficiency and overall photography experience.

Understanding Battery and Storage Options

The Canon EOS R5 Mark II is a powerful and versatile camera, designed for both beginners and professionals. To get the most out of it, it's important to understand the battery and storage options available, as these components play a crucial role in how long you can shoot and how much content you can capture. Whether you're planning a short photography session or an extended shoot, having a good grasp of battery management and storage solutions can help ensure a smooth experience with your camera. In this section, we'll take a detailed look at the battery and storage options for the Canon EOS R5 Mark II, explaining key concepts and offering tips for efficient use.

1. Battery Options for the Canon EOS R5 Mark II

The Canon EOS R5 Mark II uses the **Canon LP-E6NH** battery, which is the latest in Canon's LP-E6 battery series. The LP-E6 series has been a reliable standard for Canon cameras, and the LP-E6NH offers some improvements in capacity and performance over its predecessors. Understanding your camera's battery capabilities, how to maximize its lifespan, and when to invest in additional batteries is essential for any photographer.

a) Canon LP-E6NH Battery Overview

- **Battery Capacity**: The LP-E6NH has a higher capacity than the older LP-E6N, with 2130mAh compared to 1865mAh. This means it can store more energy, allowing for longer shooting sessions on a single charge. For beginners, this extra capacity can be a lifesaver, especially when learning how to use the camera and experimenting with different settings. For professionals, it offers extended shooting times, which is critical during events or long shoots.

- **Battery Life**: Battery life varies depending on how you use the camera. If you're primarily using the electronic viewfinder (EVF), which consumes more power, the battery may last for around 320-380 shots. However, if you're using the LCD screen, which is slightly more efficient, you might get closer to 490-500 shots per charge.

- **Compatibility**: The LP-E6NH is backward compatible with older Canon cameras that use LP-E6N or LP-E6 batteries. This is particularly helpful for professionals who may have older Canon gear and want to use the same batteries across multiple cameras. Conversely, older LP-E6N and LP-E6 batteries can also be used in the R5 Mark II, though they won't offer the same capacity or charging efficiency.

b) Charging the Battery

The Canon EOS R5 Mark II offers multiple ways to charge the LP-E6NH battery, giving you flexibility depending on your needs and shooting environment.

- **Canon LC-E6 Charger**: This is the standard wall charger included with the camera. It takes about 2.5 hours to fully charge a depleted battery, making it a reliable option for overnight charging or during breaks between shoots. Simply insert the battery into the charger, plug it into a power outlet, and let it charge.

- **USB-C Charging**: One of the newer features of the Canon EOS R5 Mark II is the ability to charge the battery inside the camera using a USB-C cable. This is incredibly convenient for on-the-go photographers who may not have access to a power outlet. You can use a

USB-C power bank or plug the camera into a computer to charge the battery while you continue shooting or reviewing images.

- **Battery Grip (BG-R10)**: For extended shooting sessions, especially for professionals, the optional BG-R10 battery grip can hold two LP-E6NH batteries, effectively doubling your battery life. This grip is ideal for wedding photographers, wildlife shooters, or anyone who doesn't want to worry about changing batteries in the middle of an important moment. It also adds an extra set of controls for vertical shooting, making it more ergonomic.

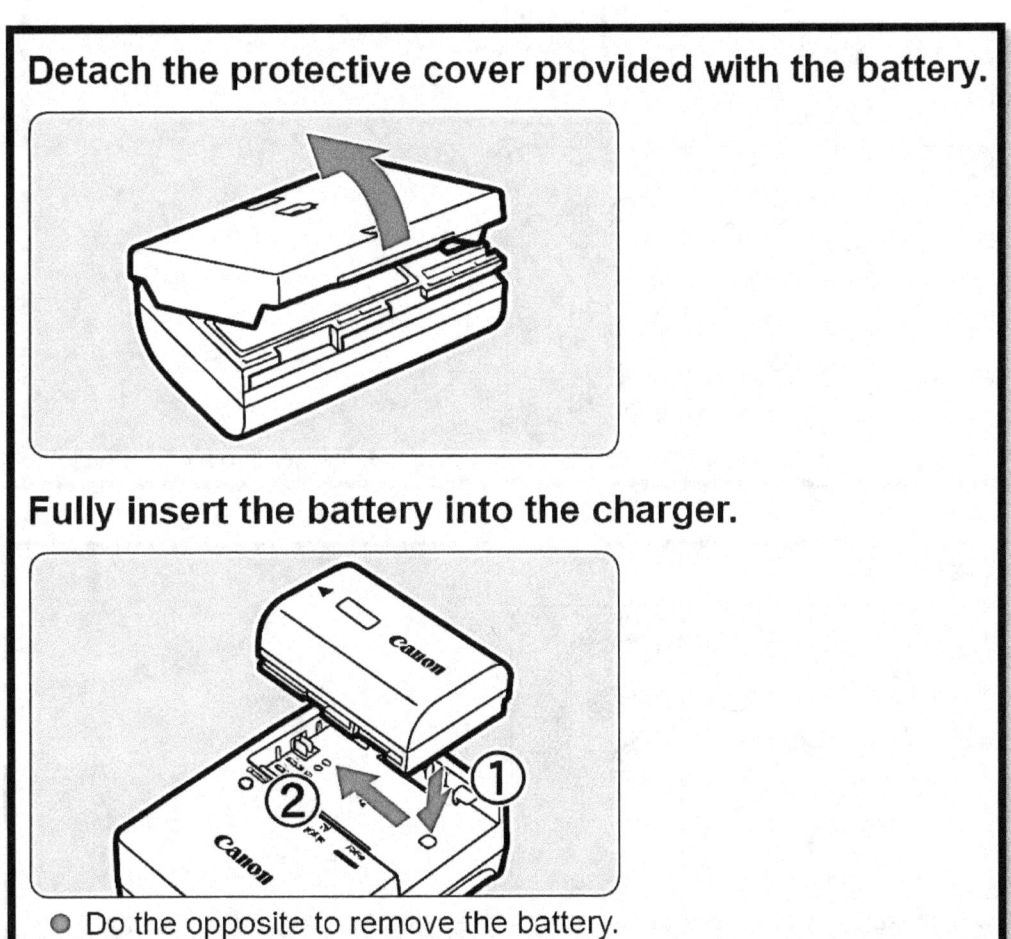

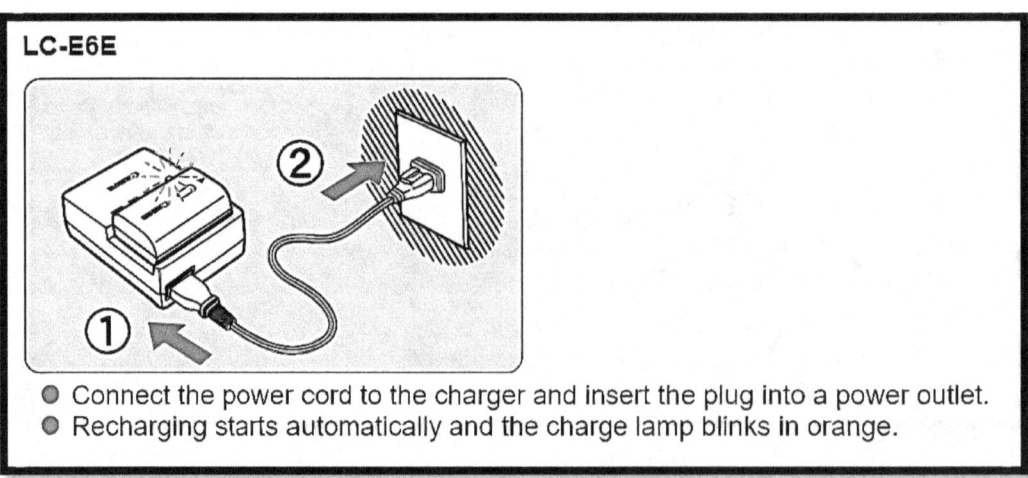

c) Battery Maintenance and Tips for Prolonging Battery Life

To get the most out of your LP-E6NH battery, it's important to follow some best practices for battery maintenance:

- **Keep Spare Batteries**: Whether you're a beginner or a professional, having at least one spare battery is always a good idea. For long shoots or when traveling, professionals may want to carry multiple fully charged batteries to avoid interruptions.

- **Avoid Extreme Temperatures**: Batteries perform best in moderate temperatures. Extreme cold can reduce battery life, while extreme heat can damage the battery over time. If you're shooting in cold conditions, keep a spare battery in a warm place, such as your pocket, and swap it out when the one in your camera starts to drain faster than usual.

- **Turn Off the Camera When Not in Use**: The R5 Mark II has excellent power-saving features, but manually turning off the camera between shots can extend battery life, especially if you're not going to shoot for a while.

- **Use Power-Saving Features**: The Canon EOS R5 Mark II offers power-saving settings, such as sleep mode, which can automatically turn off the EVF or LCD screen after a certain period of inactivity. This can help conserve battery when you're not actively shooting.

- **Firmware Updates**: Occasionally, Canon releases firmware updates that can improve battery performance. Keeping your camera's firmware up to date ensures you're getting the best possible efficiency from your battery.

2. Storage Options for the Canon EOS R5 Mark II

Just as important as your camera's battery is its ability to store the images and videos you capture. The Canon EOS R5 Mark II uses two types of memory cards: **CFexpress Type B** and **SD UHS-II** cards. Each card type has its own strengths and weaknesses, and understanding the differences can help you make the right choice for your photography or videography needs.

a) CFexpress Type B Cards

- **Speed**: CFexpress Type B cards are incredibly fast, with read and write speeds that can handle the high data demands of 8K video recording and high-speed burst shooting. If you're a professional videographer or a photographer who frequently shoots in burst mode, CFexpress cards are a must-have. They offer read speeds of up to 1700MB/s and write speeds of up to 1500MB/s, ensuring that your camera's buffer clears quickly, allowing you to keep shooting without delays.

- **Capacity**: These cards come in various capacities, ranging from 128GB to 1TB or more. For professionals shooting in 8K RAW video, the higher capacities are essential due to the large file sizes. Even for high-resolution stills, such as the 45-megapixel images produced by the Canon EOS R5 Mark II, a large-capacity CFexpress card is a good investment.

- **Durability**: CFexpress cards are designed to be robust and reliable, making them a popular choice for professionals who need to ensure that their data is safe, even in harsh shooting conditions.

b) SD UHS-II Cards

- **Speed**: While not as fast as CFexpress cards, SD UHS-II cards still offer respectable speeds, with read/write capabilities up to 300MB/s. For beginners or professionals who don't require the ultra-high performance of CFexpress, SD cards are a more affordable and practical option, especially for still photography or Full HD/4K video recording.

- **Capacity**: SD cards are available in a wide range of capacities, from 32GB to 512GB or more. For most users, a 128GB or 256GB SD card will provide ample storage for photos and 4K video. However, if you're shooting in 8K or planning to shoot a lot of video, you might want to consider higher capacity options.

- **Dual Slot Capability**: The Canon EOS R5 Mark II features two memory card slots—one for CFexpress Type B and one for SD UHS-II. This gives you flexibility in how you manage your storage. You can use both cards simultaneously, with one card serving as a backup, or you can set the camera to record stills to one card and video to another.

c) Choosing the Right Storage Option

When deciding between CFexpress and SD cards, consider the type of shooting you do:

- **For Beginners**: If you're primarily shooting still images or Full HD/4K video, SD UHS-II cards are more than sufficient. They're affordable, widely available, and offer enough speed and capacity for most casual shooting needs.

- **For Professionals**: If you're shooting high-resolution stills in burst mode, 8K video, or RAW video, CFexpress cards are a better choice due to their superior speed and capacity. Using CFexpress ensures that your camera can handle the large amounts of data generated by these demanding shooting modes without slowing down or causing delays.

d) Storage Management Tips

- **Backup Regularly**: After each shoot, it's good practice to back up your images and videos to a computer or external hard drive. This ensures that your data is safe, and it frees up space on your memory cards for your next shoot.

- **Use High-Quality Cards**: Invest in reliable, high-quality memory cards from trusted brands like Sandisk, Lexar, or Sony. Cheap or counterfeit memory cards can fail unexpectedly, resulting in data loss.

- **Label and Organize**: If you're using multiple memory cards, especially during long shoots, label your cards to avoid confusion. This is particularly helpful for professionals who may need to manage hundreds or thousands of files from a single shoot.

3. Maximizing Battery and Storage Efficiency

To ensure that you're getting the most out of your battery and storage options, here are some additional tips for both beginners and professionals:

- **Monitor Battery and Storage Levels**: The Canon EOS R5 Mark II displays both battery life and remaining storage space in the EVF and LCD screen. Keeping an eye on these indicators ensures that you won't run out of power or storage unexpectedly.

- **Turn Off Wi-Fi/Bluetooth**: If you don't need wireless connectivity, turning off Wi-Fi and Bluetooth can help extend battery life.

- **Use Lower Resolutions**: If you're not shooting for high-end professional purposes, consider using lower resolution settings (like 4K instead of 8K) or shooting in JPEG instead of RAW to save storage space and reduce battery consumption.

Conclusion

Understanding and managing the battery and storage options of the Canon EOS R5 Mark II is key to having a seamless shooting experience. Whether you're just starting out or you're a seasoned professional, knowing how to choose and manage your battery and storage setup will ensure you're always ready to capture the perfect shot.

CHAPTER 3

MASTERING PHOTOGRAPHY MODES

Auto and Scene Modes for Beginners

The Canon EOS R5 Mark II is a powerful camera, yet it's designed to help beginners get started with ease. Understanding Auto and Scene Modes is essential for new photographers, as these modes simplify the photography process by automatically adjusting key camera settings. They allow you to focus on composing your shots and capturing moments without needing a deep understanding of complex settings.

Set the shooting mode to [A⁺].

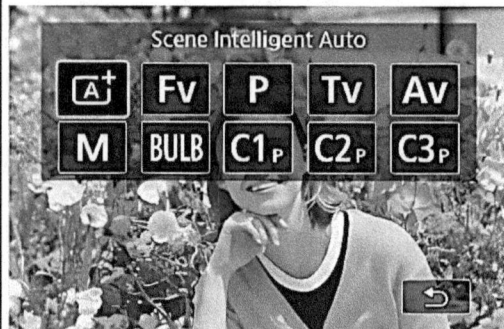

- Press the <MODE> button, then turn the <✲> dial to select [A⁺].

Aim the camera at what you will shoot (the subject).

(1)

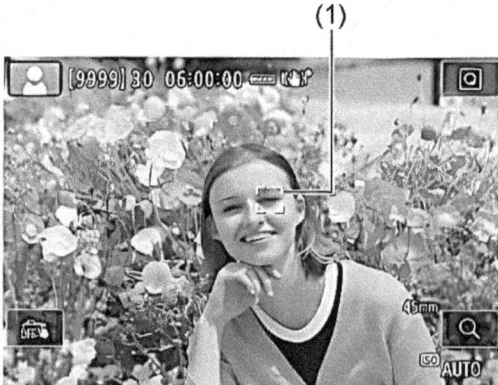

- A tracking frame (1) may be displayed on the subject, under some shooting conditions.

What Are Auto and Scene Modes?

Auto and Scene Modes on the Canon EOS R5 Mark II provide an easy entry point for beginners. These modes help you achieve great results by taking care of exposure, focus, white balance, and other settings, leaving you free to point and shoot.

Auto Mode is the simplest and most commonly used mode for beginners. It automatically adjusts everything for you, including ISO, shutter speed, aperture, white balance, and even focus. **Scene Modes** provide specialized settings tailored to particular types of photography, such as portraits, landscapes, and sports, giving your images more specific qualities suited to each subject.

Now let's dive into the details of these modes on the Canon EOS R5 Mark II.

1. Auto Mode: The All-in-One Solution

In Auto Mode, the camera acts as a "point-and-shoot" device, handling all the critical settings. Here's how it works:

- **Automatic Exposure**: The camera determines the best combination of ISO, shutter speed, and aperture for the scene. This exposure trio is essential for a balanced photo. The camera reads the available light, the subject's distance, and other factors to provide you with a well-exposed image.

- **Automatic White Balance**: White balance affects the color tone of your photos. In Auto Mode, the camera adjusts the white balance to ensure your colors appear natural, whether you're shooting indoors, outdoors, or in mixed lighting.

- **Automatic Focus**: The R5 Mark II's autofocus is fast and reliable, even in Auto Mode. It quickly locks onto subjects, whether stationary or moving, allowing you to capture sharp, clear images.

- **Automatic Flash**: In low-light conditions, the built-in flash will activate automatically if necessary, providing additional light to properly expose the scene.

How to Use Auto Mode:

- **Set the Mode Dial**: Turn the mode dial on the camera to the green "A+" symbol, which represents Auto Mode.

- **Compose Your Shot**: Frame your subject using the viewfinder or the LCD screen.

- **Press the Shutter Button Halfway**: This activates the autofocus, allowing the camera to lock onto the subject. You'll hear a beep when the camera focuses.

- **Press the Shutter Button Fully**: The camera takes the photo with all settings optimized automatically.

Benefits of Auto Mode:

- Quick and easy for beginners.
- Great for snapshots in changing lighting conditions.
- Perfect for casual photography where speed is more important than control.

2. Scene Modes: Specialized Settings for Different Situations

Scene Modes are designed for specific types of photography, and each mode adjusts the camera's settings to suit a particular scenario. The Canon EOS R5 Mark II offers various Scene Modes, such as Portrait, Landscape, Sports, and Night Scene. Let's explore each mode in detail.

Portrait Mode: Capturing People with Soft Backgrounds

Portrait Mode is ideal for photographing people. It optimizes settings to focus sharply on your subject while softly blurring the background (known as "bokeh"), making your subject stand out.

- **Wide Aperture**: The camera uses a wider aperture to create a shallow depth of field, blurring the background while keeping the subject in focus.
- **Soft Skin Tones**: It subtly adjusts color and contrast to make skin tones appear more natural.
- **Autofocus**: The camera prioritizes face detection, making it easier to capture sharp and well-exposed portraits.

Using Portrait Mode:

- **Set the Mode Dial**: Turn the mode dial to Portrait Mode, usually indicated by an icon of a person's silhouette.
- **Frame Your Subject**: Position the subject within the frame and ensure the camera is focused on their face.
- **Capture the Image**: Press the shutter button halfway to focus, then fully to take the photo.

Landscape Mode: Capturing Vivid Scenery

Landscape Mode is perfect for outdoor scenes and landscapes. It optimizes settings to capture vibrant colors and sharp details across a wide area.

- **Small Aperture**: The camera uses a smaller aperture for a larger depth of field, keeping most of the scene in focus.
- **Vibrant Colors**: Color saturation and contrast are enhanced to make skies, trees, and other landscape features appear more vivid.
- **Long Exposure**: If lighting is low, the camera may use a slower shutter speed, so using a tripod is helpful.

Using Landscape Mode:

- **Set the Mode Dial**: Switch the mode dial to Landscape Mode, typically represented by an icon of mountains.
- **Stabilize the Camera**: If possible, use a tripod to avoid camera shake, especially in low light.
- **Compose and Capture**: Frame the scene and take the photo, letting the camera handle the settings for optimal landscape quality.

Sports Mode: Freezing Fast Action

Sports Mode is tailored for capturing moving subjects. It's ideal for photographing sports, wildlife, and other fast-moving scenes where capturing a sharp image is essential.

- **Fast Shutter Speed**: The camera automatically selects a high shutter speed to freeze motion, preventing blurriness.
- **Continuous Autofocus**: It enables tracking of moving subjects, keeping them in focus as they move across the frame.
- **Burst Mode**: Sports Mode may also enable continuous shooting, allowing you to capture multiple frames in quick succession.

Using Sports Mode:

- **Set the Mode Dial**: Switch the mode dial to Sports Mode, usually represented by an icon of a running person.
- **Follow the Action**: Keep the camera aimed at your subject as they move.
- **Capture the Moment**: Press and hold the shutter button to capture a burst of images, giving you more options for selecting the best shot.

Night Scene Mode: Low-Light Photography Without Blur

Night Scene Mode is ideal for low-light environments. It helps capture night scenes and cityscapes without using a flash, preserving the natural atmosphere of the scene.

- **Long Exposure**: The camera may use a longer exposure time to allow more light into the sensor, creating a brighter image.
- **Increased ISO**: The ISO may be raised to make the camera more sensitive to light, but the camera works to minimize noise.
- **Stabilization**: The R5 Mark II's in-body image stabilization (IBIS) helps reduce blurriness caused by hand movement during long exposures.

Using Night Scene Mode:

- **Set the Mode Dial**: Turn the mode dial to Night Scene Mode, often represented by an icon of a moon or cityscape.
- **Stabilize the Camera**: Using a tripod is recommended, as long exposure times can easily lead to camera shake.
- **Frame Your Scene and Capture**: Focus on your subject or scene and take the shot, allowing the camera to optimize settings for a well-exposed nighttime photo.

Close-Up Mode (Macro): Capturing Fine Details Up Close

Close-Up Mode is perfect for photographing small subjects, like flowers, insects, or other detailed objects.

- **Wide Aperture for Soft Backgrounds**: The camera uses a wide aperture to blur the background, allowing the subject to stand out sharply.
- **Optimized Focus for Close Distances**: Close-Up Mode adjusts the focus to suit subjects that are close to the camera.

Using Close-Up Mode:

- **Set the Mode Dial**: Switch to Close-Up Mode, which is often represented by a flower icon.
- **Get Close to Your Subject**: Move the camera close to the subject, keeping enough distance to allow the lens to focus properly.
- **Capture the Details**: Press the shutter to capture the fine details of your subject with the camera's optimized settings.

Tips for Using Auto and Scene Modes

- **Learn Composition**: While the camera handles technical settings, focusing on composition (how you frame your subject) will significantly improve your photos.
- **Observe Light**: Pay attention to the lighting in your scene. Scene Modes work best in natural light, but Auto Mode will also adapt well to various lighting conditions.
- **Experiment and Practice**: Try out different Scene Modes to understand how each one impacts your photos. Practice helps you gain confidence and know which mode to use in different scenarios.

Conclusion

Auto and Scene Modes provide beginners with an accessible way to capture quality photos without the need to adjust manual settings. As you get comfortable with these modes, you'll be better prepared to explore more advanced modes, like Manual, Aperture Priority, and Shutter Priority, to gain full creative control over your photography.

Manual, Aperture, and Shutter Priority Modes

The Canon EOS R5 Mark II is a highly versatile camera that offers more than just Auto and Scene Modes. As you gain experience, you'll likely want more control over your photography. Manual, Aperture Priority, and Shutter Priority modes are powerful options that allow you to adjust key settings for greater creative flexibility. These modes enable you to control the exposure, depth of field, and motion in your images, allowing you to capture exactly what you envision.

1. Manual Mode (M): Complete Control

Manual Mode, represented by the letter "M" on the camera's mode dial, gives you full control over every setting that affects exposure: shutter speed, aperture, and ISO. Unlike Auto Mode, where the camera makes decisions for you, Manual Mode lets you determine the balance of light, motion, and focus.

Key Concepts in Manual Mode

In Manual Mode, understanding the exposure triangle—ISO, aperture, and shutter speed—is essential. Each of these settings affects your photo in specific ways:

- **ISO**: This setting controls the camera sensor's sensitivity to light. Higher ISO settings make the sensor more sensitive, useful for low-light situations but can introduce grain (noise) in the image.
- **Aperture**: Aperture refers to the size of the opening in the lens that lets light into the camera. Measured in f-stops (like f/2.8, f/5.6, f/16), a lower f-stop means a larger aperture, letting in more light and creating a shallow depth of field, ideal for portraits.

- **Shutter Speed**: This controls the duration the camera sensor is exposed to light. Faster speeds (like 1/1000) freeze motion, while slower speeds (like 1/15) create motion blur, making it great for creative effects.

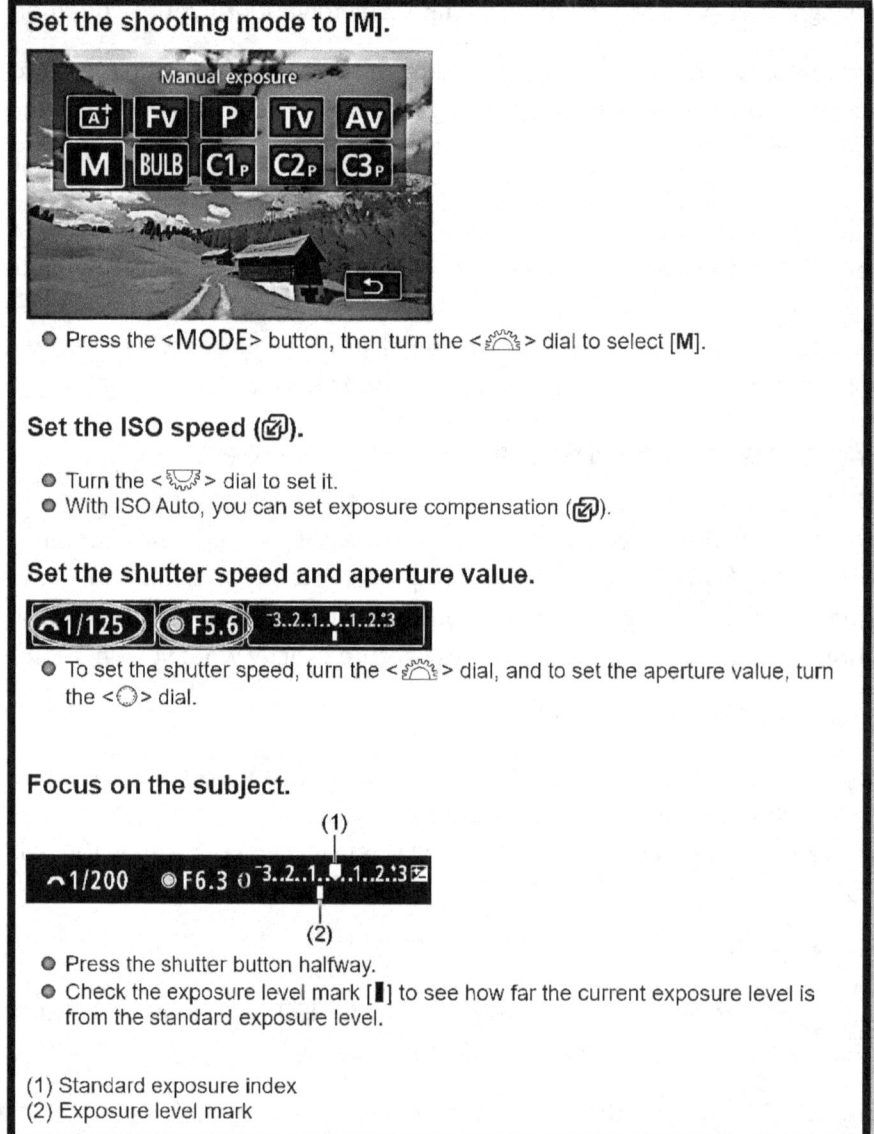

> **Set the exposure and take the picture.**
>
> ⌒1/160   ●F5.0   ⁻3..2..1..◘..1..2.⁺3
>
> ● Check the exposure level indicator and set the desired shutter speed and aperture value.

How to Use Manual Mode:

- **Set the Mode Dial to M**: Turn the camera's mode dial to "M" for Manual.

- **Adjust Aperture**: Choose your desired aperture using the camera's control dial. A low f-stop like f/2.8 will create a shallow depth of field, while a higher f-stop like f/11 keeps more of the scene in focus.

- **Set Shutter Speed**: Use the control wheel to adjust shutter speed. A fast shutter speed (like 1/500) is useful for freezing motion, while a slower shutter speed (like 1/30) captures movement.

- **Set ISO**: Adjust the ISO depending on lighting. Start with a low ISO (like 100) in bright conditions, and increase it in low light.

- **Use the Light Meter**: The camera's light meter, displayed in the viewfinder or on the screen, helps you assess exposure. Adjust the aperture, shutter speed, or ISO until the indicator is centered for balanced exposure.

- **Review Your Image**: Check the photo to see if the exposure, focus, and other elements look right. Adjust settings if needed and try again.

Benefits of Manual Mode:

- Full creative control over your images.

- Ideal for challenging lighting situations.

- Allows experimentation with exposure effects, like capturing long exposures at night.

2. Aperture Priority Mode (Av/A): Controlling Depth of Field

Aperture Priority Mode, labeled as "Av" (Aperture Value) on the Canon EOS R5 Mark II, allows you to control the aperture while the camera automatically adjusts shutter speed to maintain a balanced exposure. This mode is ideal for controlling depth of field, making it perfect for portraits, landscapes, and any scene where you want to emphasize a specific part of the image.

Set the shooting mode to [Av].

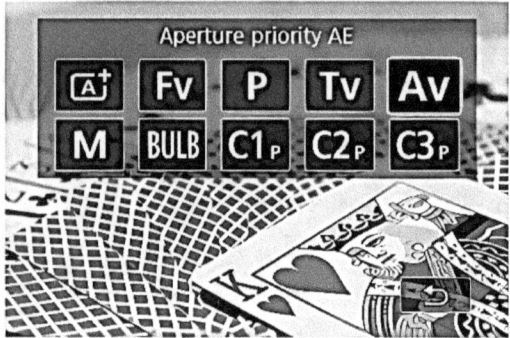

- Press the <MODE> button, then turn the <🎛> dial to select [**Av**].

Set the desired aperture value.

- Turn the <🎛> dial to set it.

Focus on the subject.

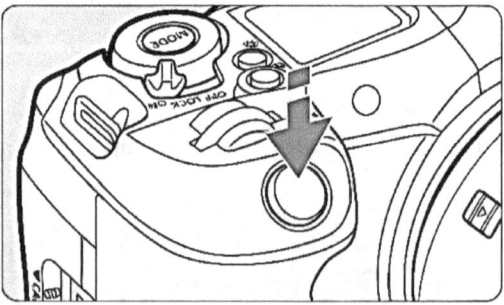

- Press the shutter button halfway.
- The shutter speed is set automatically.

Check the display and shoot.

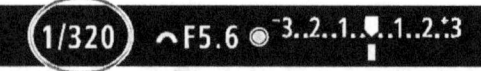

- As long as the shutter speed is not blinking, the standard exposure will be obtained.

Key Concepts in Aperture Priority Mode

Aperture Priority Mode enables you to control how much of your image is in focus by adjusting the size of the aperture.

- **Low Aperture (e.g., f/1.8, f/2.8)**: Allows more light to enter and creates a shallow depth of field, blurring the background while keeping the subject sharp. This effect is often used in portrait photography to draw attention to the subject.

- **High Aperture (e.g., f/8, f/16)**: Limits the amount of light and creates a larger depth of field, keeping more of the scene in focus. This is great for landscapes, where you want both the foreground and background to appear sharp.

How to Use Aperture Priority Mode:

- **Set the Mode Dial to Av**: Turn the mode dial to "Av" for Aperture Priority.

- **Adjust the Aperture**: Use the control dial to select the desired f-stop value. A low f-stop creates a soft background, while a high f-stop keeps more of the image in focus.

- **Set ISO**: Set the ISO manually or use Auto ISO. In bright light, use a low ISO (like 100), and in low light, consider increasing the ISO or using Auto ISO.

- **Compose and Shoot**: Frame your subject and press the shutter button. The camera will automatically select the correct shutter speed based on the aperture you set.

- **Check the Results**: Review your shot to see if the depth of field and exposure are as expected. Adjust the aperture as needed to get the desired effect.

Benefits of Aperture Priority Mode:

- Control over depth of field, making it ideal for portraits and landscapes.

- Faster adjustments in changing lighting conditions since the camera handles shutter speed.

- A versatile mode that lets you focus on composition without full manual adjustments.

3. Shutter Priority Mode (Tv/S): Capturing Motion

Shutter Priority Mode, labeled "Tv" (Time Value) on Canon cameras, lets you control the shutter speed while the camera adjusts the aperture. This mode is essential for capturing or freezing motion, making it a favorite for sports, wildlife, and action photography.

Set the shooting mode to [Tv].

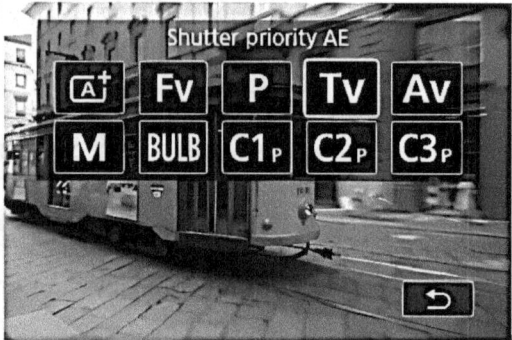

- Press the <MODE> button, then turn the <✲> dial to select [**Tv**].

Set the desired shutter speed.

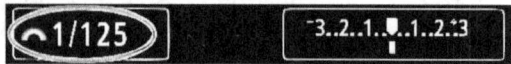

- Turn the <✲> dial to set it.

Focus on the subject.

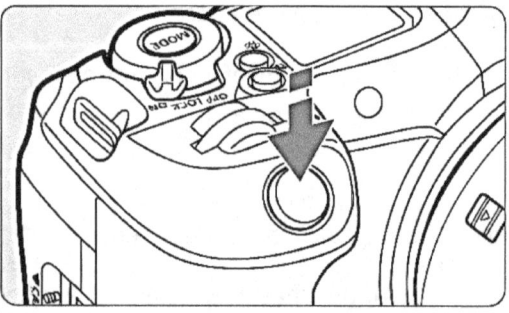

- Press the shutter button halfway.
- The aperture value is set automatically.

Check the display and shoot.

- As long as the aperture value is not blinking, the standard exposure will be obtained.

Key Concepts in Shutter Priority Mode

Shutter speed determines how long the camera's sensor is exposed to light. Adjusting shutter speed allows you to control the movement in your shots.

- **Fast Shutter Speeds (e.g., 1/1000, 1/2000)**: These settings freeze motion, ideal for capturing fast-moving subjects like athletes or animals. A faster shutter speed also reduces motion blur caused by camera shake.

- **Slow Shutter Speeds (e.g., 1/15, 1/30)**: These settings allow you to create motion blur, which can convey a sense of movement. This is useful for capturing flowing water, light trails, or creative effects in low light.

How to Use Shutter Priority Mode:

- **Set the Mode Dial to Tv**: Turn the mode dial to "Tv" for Shutter Priority.

- **Adjust the Shutter Speed**: Use the control dial to select the desired shutter speed. For example, use a speed like 1/1000 to freeze motion or 1/15 to capture motion blur.

- **Set ISO**: Manually adjust the ISO or use Auto ISO. Higher ISO can be useful in low light, especially when using fast shutter speeds.

- **Compose and Shoot**: Frame your subject and press the shutter. The camera will adjust the aperture to maintain proper exposure based on the shutter speed you set.

- **Check the Outcome**: Review the image to ensure the motion effect matches your expectations. If it doesn't, adjust the shutter speed and try again.

Benefits of Shutter Priority Mode:

- Ideal for capturing action and fast-moving subjects.

- Allows you to experiment with creative effects, like motion blur and long exposures.

- Simplifies adjustments in dynamic scenes, as the camera adjusts aperture automatically.

Putting It All Together: Choosing the Right Mode for the Right Scenario

Each of these modes—Manual, Aperture Priority, and Shutter Priority—offers different levels of control suited to different shooting situations:

- **Use Manual Mode** when you want total control over all settings. This mode is perfect for creative shots where you need specific adjustments to capture the vision you have in mind.

- **Choose Aperture Priority Mode** if you're focusing on subjects with particular depth requirements, like portraits or landscapes, where the background or foreground needs to be emphasized or de-emphasized.

- **Opt for Shutter Priority Mode** if motion is the focus, such as in sports, wildlife, or scenes with flowing water, where capturing the movement style is key.

Tips for Transitioning from Auto to Manual Modes

Switching from Auto to Manual, Aperture, or Shutter Priority modes might seem challenging, but with practice, it becomes second nature. Here are some tips:

- **Start with Aperture or Shutter Priority**: These semi-automatic modes give you creative control over either depth of field or motion without needing to manage every setting.

- **Use the Light Meter**: The R5 Mark II's light meter helps guide you in Manual Mode. Watch the exposure indicator to adjust settings accurately.

- **Practice in Different Lighting Conditions**: Try Manual Mode in various lighting environments to understand how shutter speed, aperture, and ISO interact.

- **Experiment with Different Effects**: Play with depth of field in Aperture Priority and motion effects in Shutter Priority to expand your understanding of each mode's capabilities.

- **Review and Analyze Your Photos**: Look back at your shots and note the settings used, evaluating how they affect the final image. This analysis will help you gain confidence in each mode.

Conclusion

Mastering Manual, Aperture Priority, and Shutter Priority Modes will significantly expand your photography skills. As you progress, these modes will become invaluable tools for capturing more creative, professional-looking images with your Canon EOS R5 Mark II. Practice regularly, and you'll soon harness the full power of these advanced features.

Using Bulb Mode and Advanced Settings for Professionals

The Canon EOS R5 Mark II is a camera built for creativity and precision, offering advanced settings and features for photographers who want to push the boundaries of their craft. Among these, **Bulb Mode** and other professional settings enable unique photographic opportunities like long exposures, light painting, and precise exposure control in challenging conditions. This section explores how to use Bulb Mode and advanced settings effectively, providing a step-by-step guide for professional-level photography.

1. Understanding Bulb Mode

Bulb Mode, often abbreviated as "B" in camera settings, allows the shutter to stay open for as long as the shutter button is pressed. Unlike standard shutter speeds, which max out at 30 seconds in most cameras, Bulb Mode lets you manually control the exposure time, making it ideal for long-exposure photography.

Set the shooting mode to [BULB].

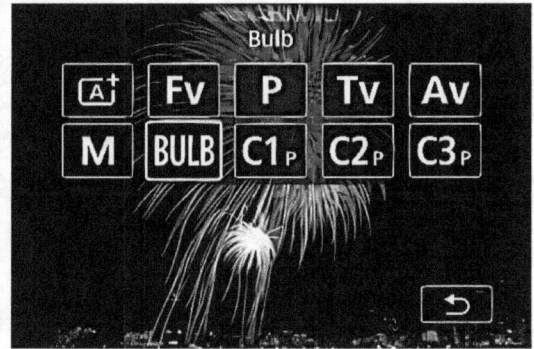

- Press the <MODE> button, then turn the < ⚙ > dial to select [BULB].

Set the desired aperture value.

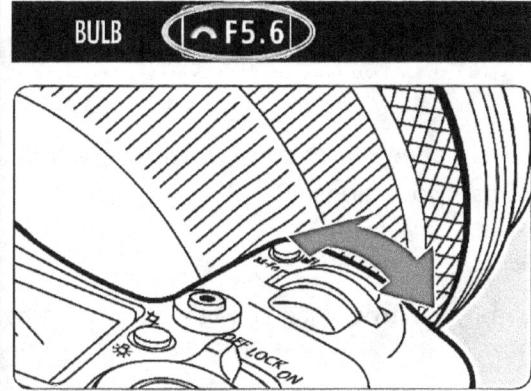

- Turn the < ⚙ > dial to set it.

Take the picture.

- The exposure will continue for as long as you keep the shutter button pressed completely.
- Elapsed exposure time is displayed on the LCD panel.

Key Applications of Bulb Mode:

- **Astrophotography**: Capture the stars, the Milky Way, or celestial events like star trails.
- **Light Painting**: Create artistic images by moving light sources in front of the camera.
- **Night Photography**: Shoot cityscapes, fireworks, or any scene in very low light.
- **Smooth Water Effects**: Create dreamy effects with waterfalls, rivers, or the ocean.

How Bulb Mode Works:

- In Bulb Mode, the camera does not set a specific shutter speed. Instead, the exposure lasts as long as the shutter button is pressed.
- This allows photographers to achieve exposure times of several seconds, minutes, or even hours.

How to Use Bulb Mode on the Canon EOS R5 Mark II:

- **Switch to Manual or Bulb Mode**:
    - Rotate the mode dial to Manual Mode ("M").
    - Set the shutter speed to **Bulb** using the control wheel.
- **Choose the Right Lens and Settings**:
    - Use a lens suitable for your subject, such as a wide-angle lens for landscapes or astrophotography.
    - Set the aperture depending on the scene. For instance, a wider aperture (like f/2.8) is ideal for capturing light in dark conditions.
- **Set ISO Sensitivity**:

    Use a low ISO (100–400) for clean, noise-free images. High ISO may introduce grain in long exposures.

- **Stabilize the Camera**:
    - Mount your R5 Mark II on a sturdy tripod to eliminate vibrations.
    - Use a remote shutter release or Canon's Camera Connect app to avoid camera shake.
- **Start and End the Exposure**:

- Press the remote shutter button or use the app to open the shutter.
- Monitor the scene's exposure and close the shutter when desired.

- **Review and Adjust**:

    Check your image for sharpness and exposure. Make adjustments to settings or timing for subsequent shots.

2. Advanced Settings for Professionals

The Canon EOS R5 Mark II offers advanced tools and settings that elevate professional photography. These features allow you to capture more dynamic images with exceptional precision.

A. Dual Pixel RAW Mode

Dual Pixel RAW is a feature that captures additional image data, enabling fine-tuning during post-processing.

Applications:

- **Micro-Adjusting Focus**: Refine focus points for sharper images.
- **Bokeh Shift**: Slightly adjust the background blur.
- **Ghosting Reduction**: Minimize ghosting effects in high-contrast scenes.

How to Use Dual Pixel RAW:

- Enable **Dual Pixel RAW** in the camera menu.
- Shoot in RAW format to preserve maximum data.
- Use Canon's Digital Photo Professional (DPP) software for post-processing adjustments.

B. Focus Bracketing and Stacking

Focus bracketing involves capturing multiple images at different focus points, which can be combined later into a single image with a greater depth of field.

Applications:

- **Macro Photography**: Ensure every detail of your subject is sharp.
- **Landscape Photography**: Maintain sharpness from the foreground to the horizon.

How to Use Focus Bracketing:

- Enable **Focus Bracketing** in the menu.
- Set the number of shots and focus increment.
- Mount the camera on a tripod for stability.
- Use software like Photoshop to merge the bracketed images.

C. Interval Timer for Time-Lapse Photography

The interval timer automates the process of capturing time-lapse sequences, which are later combined into video clips.

Applications:

- **Sunrises and Sunsets**: Capture the gradual changes in light.
- **Moving Clouds**: Create dramatic time-lapse sequences of weather patterns.

How to Use the Interval Timer:

- Enable **Interval Timer Shooting** in the menu.
- Set the interval duration (e.g., every 10 seconds) and the number of shots.
- Compose your frame and let the camera handle the rest.

D. Customizable Autofocus Settings

The advanced autofocus system in the R5 Mark II allows you to tailor settings for precise tracking and subject recognition.

Applications:

- **Sports and Wildlife**: Track fast-moving subjects with ease.
- **Portraits**: Use eye-detection autofocus for sharp focus on the eyes.

How to Customize Autofocus:

- Go to the **AF Menu** in the settings.
- Select a focus area (e.g., Spot, Zone, or Full).
- Enable **Eye Detection** for portrait work.
- Adjust tracking sensitivity for subjects moving toward or away from the camera.

3. Combining Bulb Mode and Advanced Settings

Professionals often combine Bulb Mode with advanced settings to achieve creative results. For example:

- **Light Painting with Dual Pixel RAW**: Use Bulb Mode to capture light trails, then refine focus in post-processing.

- **Star Trails with Focus Stacking**: Combine Bulb Mode for long exposures with focus stacking to ensure the foreground is sharp.

- **Time-Lapse with Manual Control**: Use manual exposure settings to ensure consistent brightness across a time-lapse sequence.

4. Tips for Using Bulb Mode and Advanced Settings

- **Plan Your Shots**: Long exposures require preparation. Scout locations, check weather conditions, and plan the duration of your exposure.

- **Use Filters**: Neutral density (ND) filters reduce light entering the lens, allowing longer exposures even in daylight.

- **Check Battery Life**: Long exposures can drain the battery quickly. Carry spare batteries or use an external power source.

- **Monitor Heat**: Extended use of Bulb Mode can cause the camera to overheat. Allow time for cooling between shots.

- **Experiment and Practice**: The more you use these settings, the more confident you'll become in achieving your creative vision.

Conclusion

Using Bulb Mode and advanced settings on the Canon EOS R5 Mark II opens a world of creative possibilities. Whether you're capturing the stars, painting with light, or shooting time-lapses, these features empower you to take your photography to the next level. With careful planning and practice, you'll harness the full potential of this remarkable camera.

CHAPTER 4

AUTOFOCUS AND EXPOSURE CONTROL

Autofocus System Overview and Settings

The Canon EOS R5 Mark II is celebrated for its cutting-edge autofocus (AF) system. Designed to provide precision, speed, and versatility, this AF system caters to a variety of shooting scenarios, from fast-paced action to intricate portraits. This section provides an in-depth overview of the autofocus system and explains how to configure it to achieve the best results.

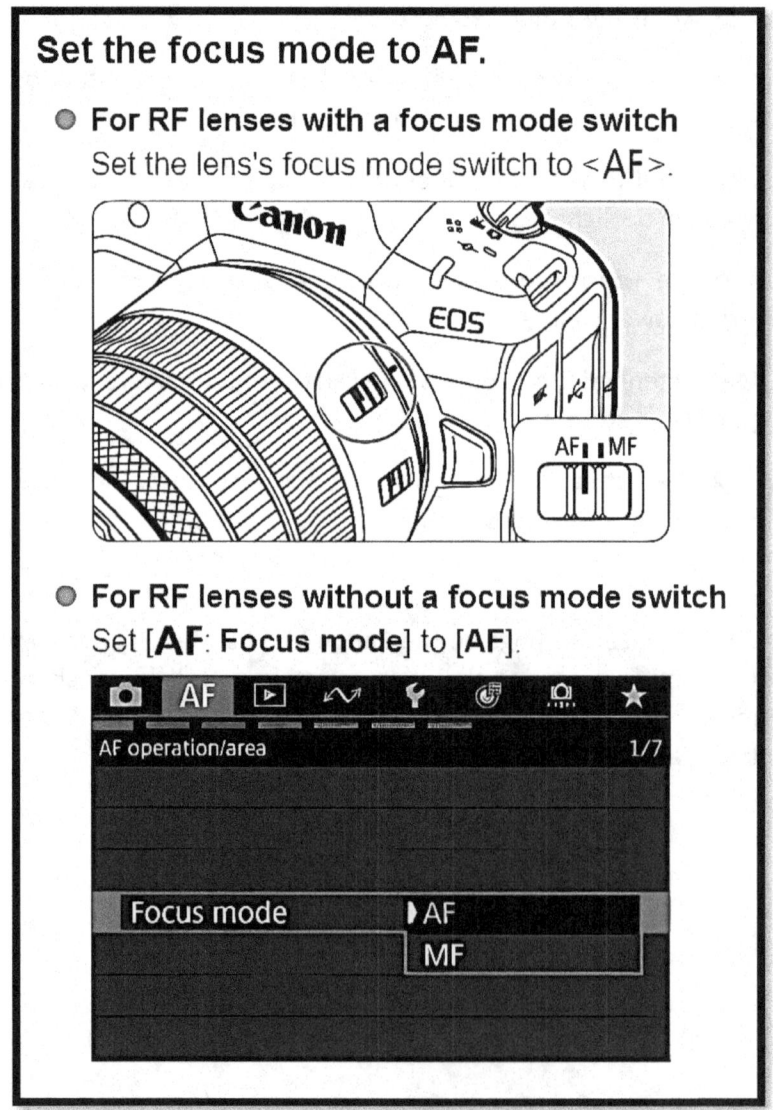

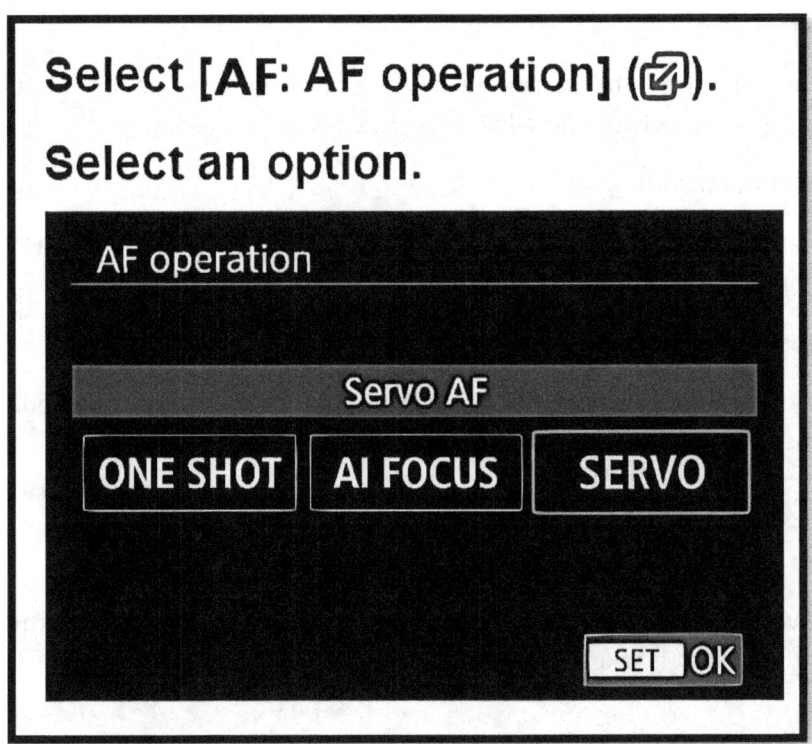

1. Overview of the Autofocus System

The EOS R5 Mark II's autofocus system is based on Canon's **Dual Pixel CMOS AF II** technology, which offers lightning-fast performance and remarkable accuracy. Here are the key highlights:

a) **Dual Pixel CMOS AF II**

This technology ensures each pixel on the sensor is used for both image capture and phase-detection autofocus. The result is smoother and more reliable focusing, especially when tracking moving subjects or shooting in low light.

b) **Subject Detection and Tracking**

The R5 Mark II can detect and track a wide range of subjects using AI-driven algorithms. Key subject-tracking features include:

- **Eye Detection AF**: Locks focus on the subject's eyes, ensuring sharp portraits.
- **Animal Detection AF**: Tracks pets and wildlife, including birds in flight.
- **Vehicle Detection AF**: Recognizes and follows cars, bikes, and other vehicles, making it ideal for motorsports photography.

c) Autofocus Coverage

With **100% coverage across the sensor** in many modes, you can focus on subjects located anywhere in the frame, offering unparalleled compositional freedom.

d) Low-Light Performance

The R5 Mark II excels in low-light scenarios, with AF sensitivity down to -6.5 EV. This makes it suitable for astrophotography and indoor shoots without additional lighting.

2. Autofocus Modes

The autofocus system in the Canon EOS R5 Mark II is versatile, offering different modes to suit various situations. Let's explore the main AF modes:

a) One-Shot AF

- **Best For**: Static subjects such as landscapes, still life, or posed portraits.
- **How It Works**: Focus locks when the shutter button is half-pressed, and the focus remains fixed until the shot is taken.

b) AI Servo AF

- **Best For**: Moving subjects like athletes, wildlife, or vehicles.
- **How It Works**: Continuously adjusts focus as the subject moves. This mode is ideal for dynamic scenarios.

c) AI Focus AF

- **Best For**: Scenarios where a subject might suddenly move, such as a child playing or an animal.
- **How It Works**: Automatically switches between One-Shot AF and AI Servo AF based on subject motion.

3. Autofocus Area Modes

The camera offers multiple area modes to customize how focus points are selected. Each mode is tailored to different needs:

a) Spot AF

- **Best For**: Pinpoint focusing on small details, such as a bird's eye or jewelry.
- **How It Works**: Focuses on a single, precise point in the frame.

b) **1-Point AF**
- **Best For**: Subjects that don't move much, like portraits or still objects.
- **How It Works**: Uses one AF point for focusing.

c) **Expand AF Area**
- **Best For**: Slightly moving subjects where focus needs a bit of flexibility.
- **How It Works**: Includes surrounding AF points to help maintain focus if the subject shifts slightly.

d) **Zone AF**
- **Best For**: Subjects that move unpredictably, such as wildlife.
- **How It Works**: Divides the frame into zones, allowing the camera to focus within a designated area.

e) **Face + Tracking AF**
- **Best For**: Portraits or moving subjects like dancers or athletes.
- **How It Works**: Automatically detects and follows faces or subjects across the frame.

4. Customizing Autofocus Settings

The Canon EOS R5 Mark II allows photographers to tailor the autofocus system to their specific needs. Customization options include:

a) **AF Speed and Sensitivity**
- Adjust the **tracking sensitivity** and **speed** to control how quickly the camera responds to changes in subject motion.
- Example: Lower sensitivity prevents the camera from shifting focus if another subject briefly enters the frame.

b) **Eye Detection AF**
- Enable this setting for automatic focus on a subject's eyes, critical for portrait photography.
- Access the setting in the **AF Menu** and choose between Human or Animal detection.

c) **Manual Selection of AF Points**

- Use the multi-controller joystick or touchscreen to manually select AF points for precise focusing.
- This is especially helpful in Spot AF or 1-Point AF modes.

d) **Focus Peaking**

- Enable focus peaking in manual focus mode to highlight areas in focus with a colored outline.
- This feature is useful for macro photography or video shooting.

5. Autofocus for Video Shooting

The R5 Mark II's autofocus capabilities extend seamlessly into video recording.

a) **Smooth Focus Transitions**

The camera allows you to control the speed of focus transitions, ensuring smooth shifts between subjects.

b) **Continuous AF in Video**

Use the **Movie Servo AF** setting to keep moving subjects in focus during video recording.

c) **Face and Eye Detection for Video**

Enable this feature to track faces or eyes for sharp focus in interviews or action scenes.

6. Troubleshooting Autofocus Issues

Even with advanced technology, autofocus may occasionally require adjustments. Here are common issues and solutions:

a) **Camera Struggles to Focus**

- **Cause**: Low light or low-contrast subjects.
- **Solution**: Use an external light source or switch to manual focus.

b) **Focus Shifts to Background**

- **Cause**: Distracting elements in the frame.
- **Solution**: Use Spot AF or 1-Point AF to target the subject precisely.

c) **Tracking Loses the Subject**

- **Cause**: Fast-moving or erratic subject motion.

- **Solution**: Adjust tracking sensitivity and use Zone AF for better coverage.

7. Practical Scenarios for Using Autofocus

a) **Wildlife Photography**

- Use **AI Servo AF** and **Animal Detection** to track animals in motion.
- Select **Zone AF** for dynamic scenes with multiple animals.

b) **Portrait Photography**

- Enable **Eye Detection AF** to ensure sharp focus on the subject's eyes.
- Use **1-Point AF** for precise control over focus placement.

c) **Sports and Action Photography**

- Combine **AI Servo AF** with **Face + Tracking** to follow athletes.
- Set a higher tracking sensitivity for rapid focus adjustments.

Conclusion

The Canon EOS R5 Mark II's autofocus system is a powerhouse of technology, designed to meet the demands of beginners and professionals alike. By understanding its modes, customizing settings, and adapting to different shooting scenarios, you can unlock the full potential of this advanced system. Mastering autofocus is an essential step toward achieving consistent, high-quality results in your photography journey.

The Exposure Triangle: ISO, Shutter Speed, and Aperture

Understanding the **Exposure Triangle** is a cornerstone of photography. It's the key to controlling the amount of light that enters your camera and affects how your images look. For the Canon EOS R5 Mark II, mastering this concept is essential to take full advantage of its advanced capabilities. The exposure triangle comprises three elements: **ISO**, **Shutter Speed**, and **Aperture**. Together, they determine the exposure of your photo while influencing its brightness, sharpness, and depth of field.

1. What is the Exposure Triangle?

The Exposure Triangle represents the interdependent relationship between ISO, shutter speed, and aperture. Adjusting one element often requires changing at least one of the others to maintain proper exposure. Here's a simple analogy: think of exposure as filling a glass of water.

- **Aperture** is the size of the tap opening (how much water flows in).

- **Shutter Speed** is the time the tap stays open (duration of the flow).
- **ISO** is the sensitivity of the container to how much water is collected (how bright the result appears).

Achieving the perfect exposure involves balancing these three elements based on your shooting scenario.

2. ISO: Light Sensitivity

ISO measures your camera sensor's sensitivity to light. The Canon EOS R5 Mark II offers a wide ISO range from **100 to 51,200**, expandable to **50 to 102,400**, catering to both bright and low-light environments.

a) Understanding ISO Values

- **Low ISO (e.g., ISO 100-400)**: Ideal for bright conditions. Produces clean images with minimal noise.
- **High ISO (e.g., ISO 1600 and above)**: Useful in dim lighting but may introduce digital noise, reducing image quality.

b) How ISO Affects Your Images

- **Brightness**: Higher ISO makes images brighter.
- **Noise**: Higher ISO can result in grainy textures.
- **Best Practice**: Always use the lowest ISO possible for your lighting conditions to minimize noise.

c) Adjusting ISO on the EOS R5 Mark II

- Press the **ISO button** on the top of the camera.
- Use the **Main Dial** to increase or decrease the ISO value.
- For convenience, enable **Auto ISO** in the menu, allowing the camera to adjust ISO automatically based on lighting.

3. Shutter Speed: Time and Motion

Shutter speed refers to how long the camera's shutter remains open, controlling the duration of light hitting the sensor. The EOS R5 Mark II offers shutter speeds ranging from **1/8000th of a second** to **30 seconds**.

a) Understanding Shutter Speed Values

- **Fast Shutter Speeds (e.g., 1/1000s and above)**: Freeze motion. Perfect for action shots, such as sports or wildlife.
- **Slow Shutter Speeds (e.g., 1/10s or slower)**: Capture motion blur. Ideal for creative effects like light trails or waterfalls.

b) **How Shutter Speed Affects Your Images**

- **Motion**: A fast shutter speed freezes motion; a slow one creates blur or streaks.
- **Light**: A longer shutter speed allows more light into the camera, useful in low-light settings.

c) **Adjusting Shutter Speed on the EOS R5 Mark II**

- In **Manual Mode (M)** or **Shutter Priority Mode (Tv)**, use the **Main Dial** to change the shutter speed.
- For action photography, use speeds like **1/2000s** to freeze fast movements.
- For long exposure photography, use a tripod and a speed like **10 seconds** to avoid camera shake.

4. Aperture: Depth and Brightness

Aperture is the size of the opening in the lens that controls the amount of light entering the camera. It's measured in **f-stops** (e.g., f/1.8, f/5.6, f/16). The EOS R5 Mark II works seamlessly with RF and EF lenses, offering a wide range of aperture settings.

a) **Understanding Aperture Values**

- **Wide Apertures (e.g., f/1.2 to f/4)**: Allow more light in, creating a shallow depth of field with blurred backgrounds.
- **Narrow Apertures (e.g., f/8 to f/22)**: Allow less light in, resulting in greater depth of field with more of the scene in focus.

b) **How Aperture Affects Your Images**

- **Light**: A wide aperture (low f-number) brightens images; a narrow aperture (high f-number) darkens them.
- **Depth of Field**: A wide aperture isolates subjects; a narrow aperture keeps everything sharp.

c) **Adjusting Aperture on the EOS R5 Mark II**

- In **Manual Mode (M)** or **Aperture Priority Mode (Av)**, use the **Quick Control Dial** to adjust the aperture.
- Experiment with wide apertures (e.g., f/2.8) for portraits and narrow ones (e.g., f/16) for landscapes.

5. Balancing the Exposure Triangle

Each element of the exposure triangle influences the others. Balancing them involves trade-offs to achieve the desired creative effect.

a) **Scenario 1: Portrait Photography**

- **Aperture**: Use a wide aperture (e.g., f/1.8) to blur the background.
- **Shutter Speed**: Use 1/125s to avoid motion blur.
- **ISO**: Keep ISO low (e.g., ISO 200) to reduce noise.

b) **Scenario 2: Action Photography**

- **Shutter Speed**: Use a fast speed (e.g., 1/2000s) to freeze motion.
- **Aperture**: Use a moderately wide aperture (e.g., f/4) to let in enough light.
- **ISO**: Increase ISO (e.g., ISO 800) to compensate for the fast shutter speed.

c) **Scenario 3: Landscape Photography**

- **Aperture**: Use a narrow aperture (e.g., f/16) for maximum depth of field.
- **Shutter Speed**: Use a slower speed (e.g., 1/30s) if the scene is static.
- **ISO**: Keep ISO low (e.g., ISO 100) for maximum image quality.

6. Using the EOS R5 Mark II's Features to Enhance Exposure Control

a) **Exposure Simulation**

The camera's electronic viewfinder (EVF) and LCD simulate exposure in real-time, helping you visualize the effects of adjustments.

b) **Histogram**

Use the histogram to evaluate exposure. A well-balanced histogram ensures highlights and shadows are not clipped.

c) **Auto Exposure Bracketing (AEB)**

Enable AEB to capture multiple shots at different exposures, allowing you to choose the best result or combine them in post-processing.

7. Troubleshooting Exposure Challenges

a) Overexposed Images

- **Cause**: Too much light entering the camera.
- **Solution**: Narrow the aperture, increase shutter speed, or lower ISO.

b) Underexposed Images

- **Cause**: Insufficient light entering the camera.
- **Solution**: Widen the aperture, decrease shutter speed, or increase ISO.

c) Unwanted Motion Blur

- **Cause**: Slow shutter speed.
- **Solution**: Use a faster shutter speed and increase ISO to compensate for reduced light.

Conclusion

The **Exposure Triangle** is the foundation of manual photography. By mastering ISO, shutter speed, and aperture, you can take full control of your Canon EOS R5 Mark II and capture images exactly as you envision them. Balancing these settings allows you to adapt to any lighting condition or creative challenge, making them indispensable tools for both beginners and professionals.

Metering Modes and Exposure Compensation

Properly exposed photographs are the foundation of professional-quality images. Achieving the right balance of brightness and detail requires a clear understanding of your camera's **metering modes** and the use of **exposure compensation**. The Canon EOS R5 Mark II provides advanced tools to measure light and adjust exposure to suit different shooting conditions. This chapter explores these concepts, ensuring you can handle any lighting scenario with confidence.

1. Understanding Metering Modes

Metering modes determine how your camera measures light in a scene. The Canon EOS R5 Mark II uses its advanced sensor and algorithms to evaluate brightness levels and suggest the best exposure settings. These modes are crucial for adapting to different lighting conditions and creative needs.

Setting from the Quick Control screen

1. **Press the <Q> button** (⊙10).
   - With an image displayed on the screen, press the <Q> button.

2. **Select the metering mode.**

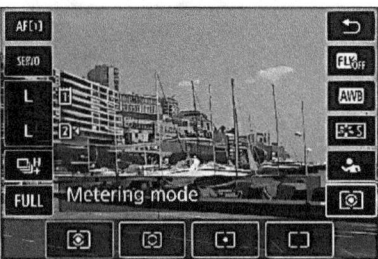

   - To select an item, turn the <○> dial or press <✻> up or down.
   - To select the metering mode, turn the <🖉> or <🖉> dial, or press <✻> left or right.

Setting from the menu

1. Select [⚫: Metering mode] (🗐).
2. Select the metering mode.

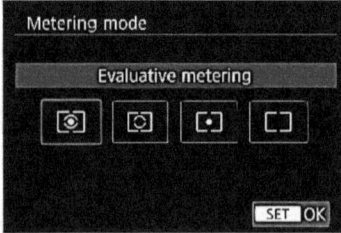

⊛ Evaluative metering

General-purpose metering mode suited even for backlit subjects. The camera adjusts the exposure automatically to suit the scene.

⊙ Partial metering

Effective where there are much brighter lights around the subject due to backlight, etc.

⊡ Spot metering

Effective when metering a specific part of the subject. The spot metering area is indicated on the screen.

▢ Center-weighted average

The metering across the screen is averaged, with the center of the screen weighted more heavily.

a) **Types of Metering Modes on the EOS R5 Mark II**

The camera offers several metering modes, each suited to specific scenarios:

- **Evaluative Metering (Default Mode)**
    - **What It Does**: Measures light across the entire frame, prioritizing the area around the focus point.
    - **When to Use It**: Ideal for general photography, including landscapes and portraits.
    - **Why It's Helpful**: Balances light from multiple areas, ensuring proper exposure in most situations.

- **Spot Metering**
    - **What It Does**: Measures light from a small area (approx. 3.1% of the frame) around the selected focus point.
    - **When to Use It**: Useful for high-contrast scenes where precise exposure control is needed, such as shooting a backlit subject.
    - **Why It's Helpful**: Gives you control over a specific part of the frame without considering the rest.

- **Partial Metering**
    - **What It Does**: Measures light from a slightly larger area (approx. 6.1% of the frame) around the center.
    - **When to Use It**: Effective for scenes with bright backgrounds, such as portraits against a sunset.
    - **Why It's Helpful**: Provides better control than evaluative metering but is less restrictive than spot metering.

- **Center-Weighted Average Metering**
    - **What It Does**: Prioritizes the center of the frame while averaging light across the entire scene.
    - **When to Use It**: Good for evenly lit scenes where the subject is centered, such as group photos.
    - **Why It's Helpful**: Balances subject and background exposure while favoring the main subject.

b) **How to Select and Adjust Metering Modes**

- Press the **Q button** or access the Quick Control screen.
- Navigate to the **Metering Mode** icon.
- Use the Multi-Controller or touchscreen to select your desired mode.

2. Mastering Exposure Compensation

While metering modes provide a baseline for exposure, some situations require manual adjustments to achieve the desired result. This is where **exposure compensation** comes in. It allows you to make the image brighter or darker by overriding the camera's metering system.

a) **What is Exposure Compensation?**

- Measured in **stops**, exposure compensation lets you increase (+) or decrease (−) the brightness of your photo.
- The EOS R5 Mark II allows for adjustments in **⅓-stop increments**, with a range typically from **−3 to +3 stops**.

b) **When to Use Exposure Compensation**

- **High-Contrast Scenes**

Example: A snowy landscape often looks too dark because the camera tries to average the brightness. Increase exposure compensation (+1 to +2 stops) to preserve the scene's brightness.

- **Backlit Subjects**

Example: A subject with strong light behind them may appear underexposed. Use positive exposure compensation to brighten the subject.

- **Low-Light Environments**

Example: Dimly lit interiors may need slight adjustments to enhance shadow details.

- **Creative Effects**

Example: Deliberately underexpose (-1 stop) for moody silhouettes or overexpose (+1 stop) for a dreamy effect.

c) **How to Use Exposure Compensation on the EOS R5 Mark II**

- Set the camera to **Aperture Priority (Av)**, **Shutter Priority (Tv)**, or **Program Auto (P)** mode.

- Locate the **Exposure Compensation Dial** or use the Quick Control screen.
- Rotate the dial or use the touchscreen to adjust exposure compensation. Watch the exposure indicator in the viewfinder or LCD for feedback.

3. Combining Metering Modes and Exposure Compensation

To handle complex lighting conditions, you'll often need to use both metering modes and exposure compensation together.

a) **Scenario 1: Bright and Backlit Scenes**
- **Problem**: A person standing in front of a bright window appears as a silhouette.
- **Solution**:
    - Switch to **Spot Metering** to measure light on the subject.
    - Use **+1 to +2 stops** of exposure compensation to brighten their face.

b) **Scenario 2: Sunset Photography**
- **Problem**: The sky looks too bright, and the colors are washed out.
- **Solution**:
    - Use **Partial Metering** to measure light near the horizon.
    - Apply **-1 stop** of exposure compensation to deepen the colors.

c) **Scenario 3: Shooting in Snow**
- **Problem**: The snow appears gray instead of white.
- **Solution**:
    - Use **Evaluative Metering** to measure the scene.
    - Apply **+1 to +1.5 stops** of exposure compensation to correct the snow's brightness.

4. Advanced Techniques with the EOS R5 Mark II

a) **Highlight Alert and Zebra Patterns**

Enable **Highlight Alert** or **Zebra Patterns** to detect overexposed areas in real time. These tools can guide your exposure adjustments.

b) **Exposure Lock (AE Lock)**

Use the **AE Lock button** to lock the current exposure settings, allowing you to recompose the shot without altering the exposure.

c) **Auto Exposure Bracketing (AEB)**

- Capture multiple exposures of the same scene by enabling **AEB** in the settings.
- This is especially useful for HDR photography, where you combine underexposed, properly exposed, and overexposed shots.

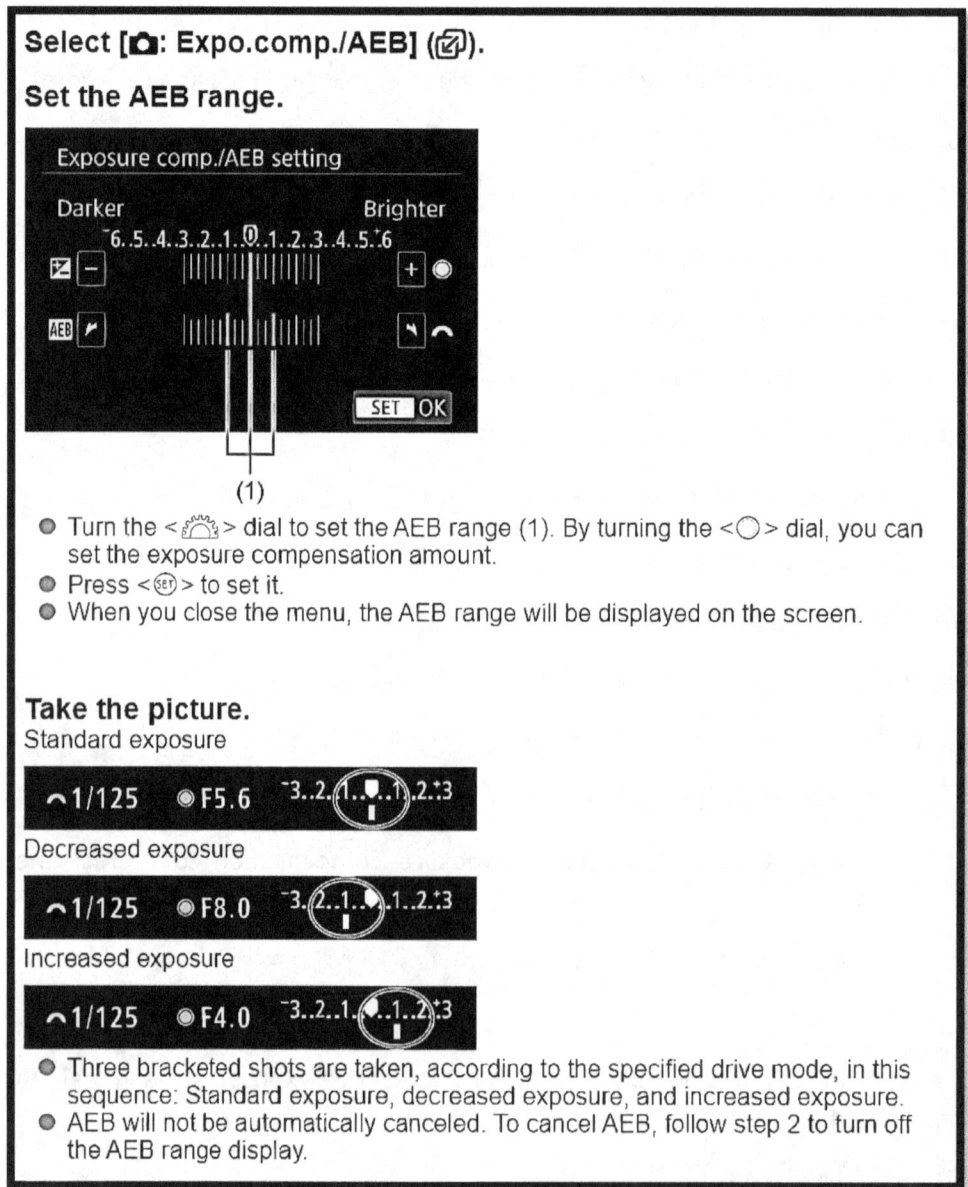

5. Tips for Mastering Metering Modes and Exposure Compensation

- **Understand Your Scene**

    Before choosing a metering mode, assess the scene's lighting and decide which areas are most important to expose correctly.

- **Practice Makes Perfect**

    Experiment with different metering modes and exposure compensation settings in a variety of lighting conditions to develop confidence.

- **Use the Live View and Histogram**

    The EOS R5 Mark II's live view shows real-time exposure adjustments. The histogram provides a graphical representation of light and shadow balance.

- **Use RAW Format**

    Shooting in RAW allows greater flexibility in post-processing to correct exposure errors.

Conclusion

Mastering **metering modes** and **exposure compensation** on the Canon EOS R5 Mark II is essential for capturing stunning photographs in any lighting condition. These tools provide precise control over how your camera interprets light, ensuring your creative vision translates into beautifully exposed images. By practicing these techniques and leveraging the camera's advanced features, both beginners and professionals can elevate their photography to new heights.

CHAPTER 5

WORKING WITH LENSES

Lens Compatibility: RF vs. EF Lenses

When using the Canon EOS R5 Mark II, understanding lens compatibility is crucial for getting the best out of your camera. Canon lenses primarily come in two types that users will encounter: RF and EF lenses. This section will guide beginners and professionals through the differences, benefits, and how to use each type effectively with the EOS R5 Mark II.

1. Introduction to Canon Lens Mounts

The Canon EOS R5 Mark II uses Canon's RF mount, a modern design that's optimized for mirrorless cameras. It also has compatibility with EF lenses, which are part of Canon's legacy system for DSLR cameras. Understanding these mounts can help you choose the right lens for various photography and videography needs.

- **RF Mount**: Introduced with Canon's transition to mirrorless systems, the RF mount supports new, technologically advanced RF lenses.

- **EF Mount**: The older, well-established mount used for Canon's DSLR cameras, supporting a vast array of EF and EF-S lenses.

Let's break down each type of lens and explain how they work with the Canon EOS R5 Mark II.

2. What is the RF Mount?

Canon's RF mount is designed specifically for its mirrorless series, starting with the EOS R lineup. It features a short flange distance (the distance between the sensor and the lens mount), allowing lenses to be closer to the sensor. This design change offers several advantages:

- **Improved Image Quality**: The shorter flange distance enables lens elements to be placed closer to the sensor, reducing optical distortions and enhancing image quality, especially at the edges of the frame.

- **Innovative Lens Design**: RF lenses incorporate advanced optical technologies, such as built-in control rings for customizable settings. This feature allows photographers to adjust aperture, ISO, or exposure compensation directly on the lens, streamlining workflow.

- **Better Communication**: The RF mount has a higher data transfer rate between the camera and lens, facilitating faster autofocus, more accurate stabilization, and better overall lens performance.

The Canon EOS R5 Mark II, with its sophisticated sensor and processor, pairs seamlessly with RF lenses to provide exceptional performance.

Popular RF Lenses for the EOS R5 Mark II:

- **Canon RF 24-70mm f/2.8L IS USM**: A versatile, high-quality zoom lens perfect for everything from landscapes to portraits.

- **Canon RF 50mm f/1.2L USM**: A premium prime lens known for its superior sharpness and low-light performance.

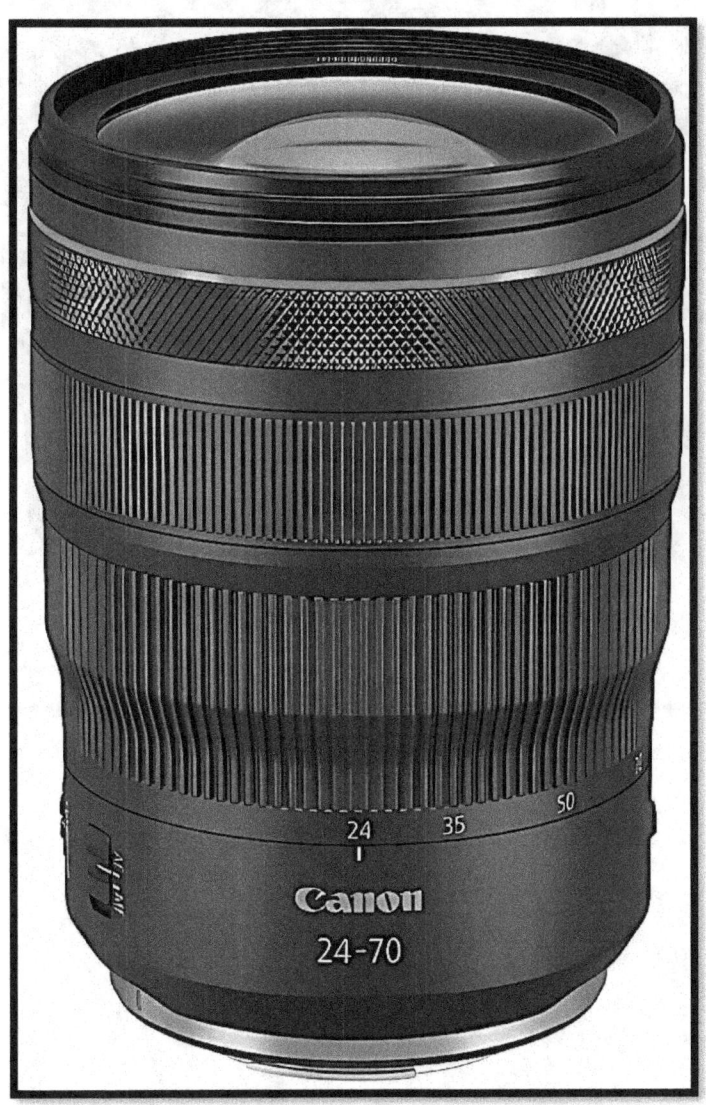

Canon RF 24-70mm f/2.8L IS USM

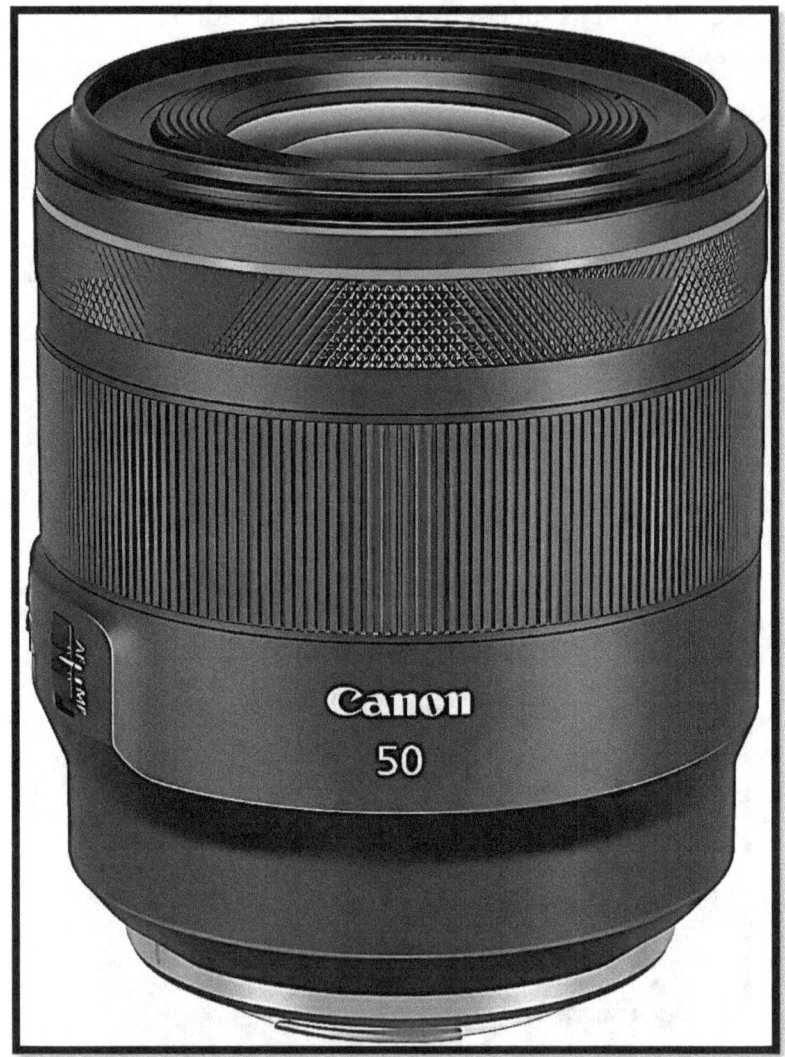

Canon RF 50mm f/1.2L USM

Pros of RF Lenses:

- Optimized for modern mirrorless sensors.
- Faster and more reliable autofocus.
- Enhanced optical features like image stabilization and control rings.

Cons of RF Lenses:

- Higher cost compared to many EF lenses.

- Limited variety in comparison to the vast EF lens lineup (though this is expanding).

3. What is the EF Mount?

The EF (Electro-Focus) mount has been around since 1987, serving as the foundation for Canon's extensive DSLR lens system. It's compatible with both full-frame and APS-C (EF-S) lenses, though only full-frame EF lenses are recommended for use with the EOS R5 Mark II to ensure full coverage of the sensor.

Key Characteristics of EF Lenses:

- **Wide Range of Options**: The EF mount boasts one of the most extensive collections of lenses, from budget-friendly options to high-end L-series professional lenses.
- **Adaptability**: The EOS R5 Mark II can use EF lenses through the use of a Canon EF-EOS R mount adapter. This allows photographers who have invested in EF lenses to use them with their mirrorless camera.

Advantages of Using EF Lenses:

- **Cost-Effective**: EF lenses, especially older models, are generally more affordable than newer RF lenses.
- **Specialized Lenses**: EF lenses include a variety of specialized options such as tilt-shift and ultra-telephoto lenses that may not yet be available in RF versions.

Cons of EF Lenses on Mirrorless Cameras:

- May be bulkier due to the need for an adapter.
- Potentially slower autofocus compared to native RF lenses, especially in video mode.

4. Using the Canon EF-EOS R Adapter

One of the standout features of Canon's mirrorless system is its compatibility with EF lenses through the EF-EOS R adapter. This small but powerful accessory acts as a bridge, enabling seamless integration of EF lenses with RF-mount cameras like the EOS R5 Mark II.

Benefits of the Adapter:

- **Preserved Functionality**: Autofocus, image stabilization, and aperture control are fully supported, ensuring that the lenses perform as they would on a DSLR.
- **Extended Life of Lenses**: The adapter lets photographers leverage their existing EF lens collection, making the switch to mirrorless more economical.

- **Additional Control Features**: Some versions of the adapter come with built-in control rings, adding functionality similar to RF lenses.

Types of Adapters:

- **Standard EF-EOS R Adapter**: A basic adapter for using EF lenses with no additional features.
- **Control Ring Mount Adapter**: Includes a customizable control ring, providing extra convenience for adjusting camera settings.
- **Drop-In Filter Mount Adapter**: This unique version allows the use of drop-in filters, ideal for photographers needing built-in ND or polarizing filters for creative work.

Tips for Using the Adapter:

- Ensure that firmware on both the camera and the adapter is up-to-date to maintain optimal compatibility and performance.
- Be mindful of any slight shifts in weight distribution, as using larger EF lenses can make the camera front-heavy.

5. Comparing Performance: RF vs. EF Lenses on the EOS R5 Mark II

Autofocus and Speed:

- **RF Lenses**: Benefit from the enhanced communication speed of the RF mount, leading to faster and more precise autofocus, crucial for action and wildlife photography.
- **EF Lenses with Adapter**: Perform admirably, though autofocus can sometimes be marginally slower, particularly in low-light conditions or when tracking moving subjects.

Image Quality:

- **RF Lenses**: Optimized for the full capabilities of mirrorless sensors, they often produce sharper images with better edge-to-edge clarity.
- **EF Lenses**: Still produce excellent images but may exhibit minor vignetting or softness at the corners, especially when older lenses are used.

Ergonomics and Handling:

- **RF Lenses**: Generally more compact due to the mirrorless design, making the overall setup lighter and more balanced.
- **EF Lenses with Adapter**: The adapter adds to the length, potentially impacting the center of balance, which can be an issue when hand-holding the camera for long periods.

Price Considerations:

- RF lenses are typically more expensive due to newer technology and higher manufacturing costs.
- EF lenses provide budget-friendly options, particularly for those transitioning from DSLR systems.

6. Deciding Which Lens System to Use

For Beginners:

Recommendation: Start with a versatile RF lens like the Canon RF 24-105mm f/4L IS USM for a balance of quality and ease of use. If budget is a concern, explore EF lenses with an adapter to take advantage of more affordable choices.

For Professionals:

Recommendation: Invest in RF lenses to fully leverage the high-resolution sensor and cutting-edge features of the EOS R5 Mark II. This ensures the best autofocus performance and image quality. However, using specialized EF lenses like tilt-shift or macro lenses via the adapter can also be valuable.

Long-Term Strategy:

Consider gradually transitioning to RF lenses as Canon expands its lineup. While EF lenses remain a solid option, RF lenses provide a future-proof choice aligned with the latest advancements in optical technology.

Conclusion

Both RF and EF lenses have their strengths and ideal use cases when paired with the Canon EOS R5 Mark II. RF lenses shine with their optimized designs, fast communication, and enhanced image quality, making them ideal for those who seek the utmost in performance. EF lenses, adaptable with the help of an adapter, offer a cost-effective alternative with a broad selection, suitable for photographers transitioning from older DSLR setups or needing specialized lenses.

By understanding the compatibility, benefits, and trade-offs of each lens type, users can make informed choices that best suit their photography needs and budget.

Focusing Techniques for Sharp Images

Achieving sharp images with the Canon EOS R5 Mark II requires understanding and applying the right focusing techniques. This is important whether you're capturing portraits, action shots, or detailed landscapes. This section will break down key focusing techniques suitable for both beginners and professionals, ensuring you get the most from your camera's powerful autofocus system and manual focus capabilities.

1. Understanding the Autofocus System

The Canon EOS R5 Mark II boasts an advanced autofocus (AF) system that includes Dual Pixel CMOS AF II technology, which offers rapid and precise focusing. This system is designed to track and maintain focus on subjects, even in challenging conditions. Here's what beginners and professionals need to know:

- **AF Points and Areas**: The camera features a wide range of AF points, covering most of the frame. This makes it easier to maintain focus on off-center subjects without recomposing your shot.

- **Eye Detection AF**: The EOS R5 Mark II can detect and lock focus on the eyes of people and animals. This feature is invaluable for portrait and wildlife photography, ensuring the eyes—often the focal point of an image—are sharp.

- **AI Servo AF vs. One-Shot AF**:
    - **AI Servo AF**: Continuous autofocus that tracks moving subjects. Ideal for sports, wildlife, or any situation where the subject is in motion.
    - **One-Shot AF**: Suitable for static subjects like landscapes or portraits. Once focus is achieved, the camera locks the focus, allowing for precise recomposition if needed.

Tips for Using the Autofocus System:

- **Select the Right AF Area Mode**: Use "Spot AF" for pinpoint precision or "Zone AF" for tracking a subject within a larger area.

- **Customize AF Settings**: The EOS R5 Mark II allows you to fine-tune AF settings, such as sensitivity and tracking speed. Adjust these according to your shooting scenario to optimize performance.

2. Mastering Manual Focus

While the autofocus system in the Canon EOS R5 Mark II is powerful, there are times when manual focus (MF) is preferable. This is particularly true for macro photography, low-light scenes, or when working with lenses that might not have fast AF capabilities.

How to Use Manual Focus:

- **Focus Peaking**: This feature highlights the areas in focus with a bright color overlay, helping you see where the sharpest focus lies. Adjust the color and sensitivity to match your preferences for clear visibility.
- **Magnification Tool**: The EOS R5 Mark II allows you to magnify the viewfinder or LCD screen to fine-tune focus, which is especially useful for intricate compositions.
- **Lens Control Ring**: On some RF lenses, the control ring can be set to assist with manual focusing, providing tactile feedback that aids in precision.

Tips for Effective Manual Focusing:

- **Stabilize Your Camera**: Using a tripod or steady surface can reduce the risk of slight movements that blur your shot.
- **Combine with Focus Peaking**: Activate focus peaking to confirm the critical focus area without straining your eyes.

3. Selecting the Right Focus Mode for Your Scene

The EOS R5 Mark II offers several focusing modes tailored to different shooting scenarios. Selecting the right one can dramatically improve your image sharpness:

- **Single-Point AF**: Allows you to select a specific focus point, perfect for still subjects where precise focusing is required, such as portrait photography.
- **Expand AF Area**: Uses a main focus point with surrounding points as assistance. This is great for subjects that might move slightly within the frame, like animals or street photography.
- **Tracking AF**: Automatically follows a subject as it moves across the frame. This is especially useful for capturing erratic movements, such as in sports or wildlife photography.

Practical Example: For action photography, set the camera to "AI Servo AF" with "Tracking AF" enabled. Select an initial AF point to start tracking your subject, and let the camera's intelligent system follow the motion.

4. Using Focus Lock and Recompose Technique

Sometimes, you want to compose a shot where the subject is off-center. The focus lock and recompose technique helps you achieve this without losing focus:

Step-by-Step Process:

- **Select One-Shot AF** and set your focus point on your subject (e.g., a person's eyes).
- **Half-press the shutter button** to lock the focus.
- **Recompose the shot** by adjusting the framing while maintaining the half-press.
- **Fully press the shutter button** to take the photo.

Advantages of This Technique:

- Allows creative compositions while maintaining sharp focus.
- Reduces the need for constant AF point changes.

Cautions:

Be mindful of depth-of-field changes as you recompose. If you move too much, your focus point could shift slightly.

5. Achieving Sharpness with Depth of Field

Understanding and controlling depth of field (DoF) is essential for achieving sharp images:

- **Aperture Selection**:
    - **Wide Apertures (e.g., f/2.8, f/1.4)**: Create a shallow DoF, ideal for portraits where the subject is in sharp focus while the background is blurred.
    - **Narrow Apertures (e.g., f/11, f/16)**: Increase DoF, making more of the scene in focus. This is suitable for landscape photography.
- **Hyperfocal Distance**: For landscape shots where you want both foreground and background sharp, use the hyperfocal distance technique. This means focusing at a specific point where the DoF extends from half that distance to infinity.

Tips:

- Use the depth of field preview button on the camera to see how much of the scene will be in focus before you take the shot.
- Pair narrow apertures with a tripod to avoid camera shake due to slower shutter speeds.

6. Practical Techniques for Action and Low-Light Scenarios

Capturing Motion (Sports, Wildlife):

- **Use High ISO and Fast Shutter Speeds**: In fast-moving scenes, a higher ISO allows for quicker shutter speeds, preventing motion blur.
- **Set to AI Servo AF and High-Speed Continuous Shooting**: This ensures the camera continuously refocuses on the moving subject while capturing a series of shots.

Shooting in Low Light:

- **Enable AF Assist Beam**: This feature helps the camera lock focus in dimly lit environments by projecting a beam of light.
- **Use Wide Apertures**: Letting in more light aids the autofocus system and helps maintain sharp focus.
- **Manual Focus with Focus Peaking**: In extremely low light, autofocus may struggle. Switching to manual focus and enabling focus peaking can provide better results.

7. Advanced Professional Techniques

Back-Button Focusing: This technique involves assigning focus activation to a button on the back of the camera, separate from the shutter release. The benefit is greater control over when and how focus is achieved:

Benefits:

- Prevents accidental refocusing when pressing the shutter button.
- Ideal for tracking a moving subject continuously or holding focus between shots.

How to Set Up Back-Button Focusing:

- Go to the camera's custom functions menu.
- Assign AF-ON or another rear button to control focus.
- Set the shutter button to only release the shutter, not control focus.

Combining with AI Servo AF: Back-button focusing is highly effective when combined with continuous AF modes for wildlife or sports, where you need to keep tracking but may want to momentarily stop focusing without releasing the shutter button.

Micro-Adjusting Autofocus: For professionals seeking pinpoint accuracy, calibrating lenses using micro-adjustment settings ensures optimal performance, especially with third-party or older lenses.

Steps for AF Micro-Adjustment:

- Set up a focus target at a known distance.

- Take test shots and review sharpness.
- Adjust the AF micro-adjustment setting incrementally until sharpness is maximized.

Conclusion

Achieving sharp images with the Canon EOS R5 Mark II involves mastering both autofocus and manual focusing techniques, understanding depth of field, and applying practical methods for different scenarios. By selecting the appropriate focusing mode and making adjustments based on your shooting conditions, you can consistently capture high-quality, crisp images whether you're a beginner or an experienced professional.

Using Lens Accessories (Filters, Hoods, Extenders)

Accessories can transform your photography by enhancing the capabilities of your Canon EOS R5 Mark II. This section explains the use of filters, lens hoods, and extenders—three essential accessories that can elevate your images. Each is detailed for both beginners and professionals to understand their benefits and how to use them effectively.

1. Filters: Types and Their Uses

Filters are thin, often glass or resin attachments that screw onto the front of your lens or are inserted into a holder system. They alter how light enters the lens and can achieve different effects.

Common Types of Filters:

- **UV Filters**: These are primarily used to protect the front element of the lens. While older film cameras needed them to reduce ultraviolet haze, modern digital sensors do not benefit as much. However, they still serve as an excellent way to protect your expensive lenses from dust, smudges, and scratches.

- **Polarizing Filters**: Circular polarizers help reduce glare from reflective surfaces like water and glass, deepen blue skies, and enhance color saturation. This is particularly useful for landscape photography.

- **Neutral Density (ND) Filters**: ND filters reduce the amount of light that reaches the sensor without affecting the color of the image. They allow for longer exposures in bright conditions, enabling effects like smooth water in waterfalls or motion blur in clouds.

- **Graduated ND Filters**: These are similar to ND filters but have a gradient that transitions from dark to clear. They're great for balancing exposure in scenes where the sky is much brighter than the foreground.

- **Special Effects Filters**: These include filters for color correction, starburst effects, and soft focus.

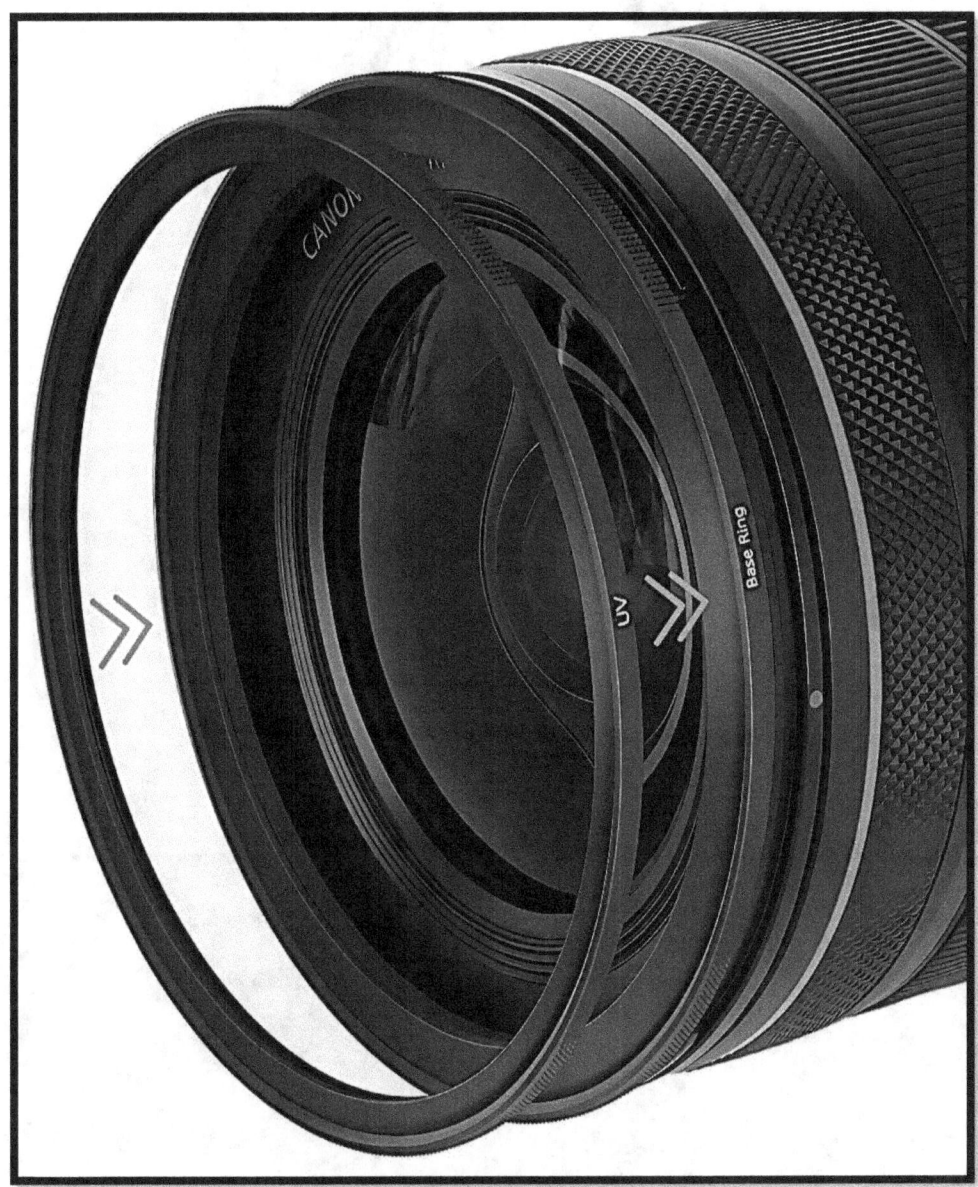

UV Filters

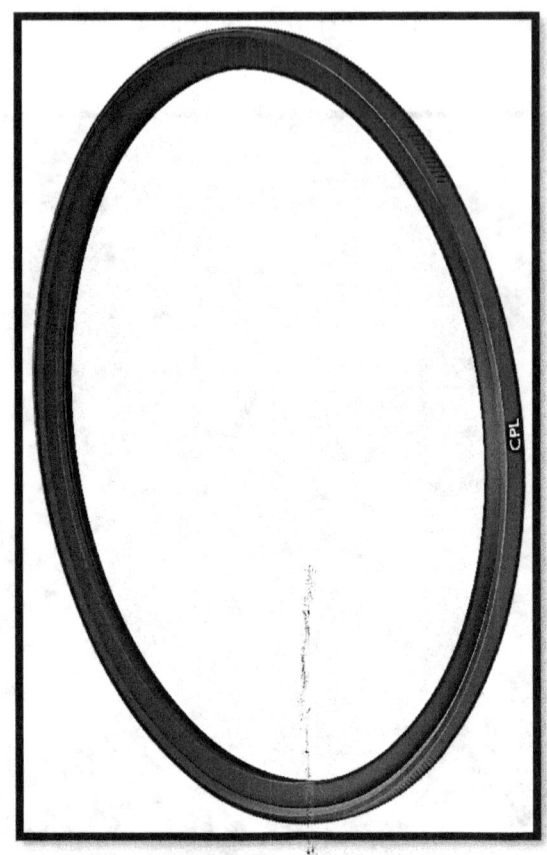

Polarizing Filters

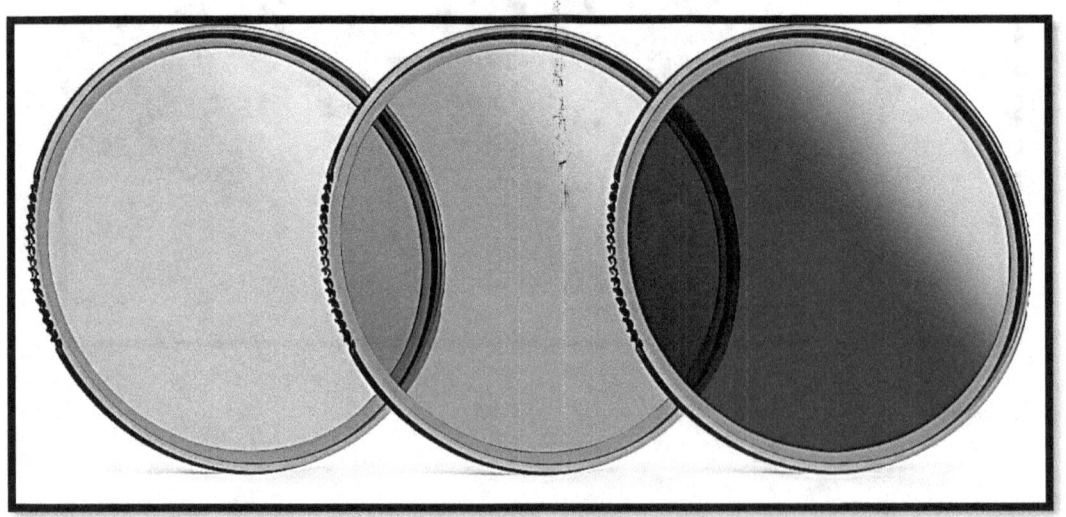

Neutral Density (ND) Filters

How to Use Filters:

- **Attaching a Filter**: Simply screw the filter onto the front thread of your lens. For more complex filters like graduated ND filters, you may use a filter holder system.
- **Stacking Filters**: While stacking can increase versatility (e.g., using a polarizer with an ND filter), be mindful of potential vignetting, especially on wide-angle lenses.

Tips for Beginners:

- Start with a polarizing filter, as it provides immediate benefits in outdoor photography.
- Invest in high-quality filters to avoid image degradation. Cheap filters can introduce unwanted reflections or reduce sharpness.

Advanced Techniques for Professionals:

- Combine different ND filters to achieve precise control over exposure, such as using a 10-stop ND filter for extremely long exposures in daylight.
- Experiment with polarizing filters to cut through haze and reflections when photographing cityscapes or nature scenes.

2. Lens Hoods: Why and When to Use Them

A lens hood is an accessory that attaches to the front of your lens and extends outward. Its primary purpose is to block stray light from entering the lens, which reduces lens flare and increases contrast.

Benefits of Using Lens Hoods:

- **Reduced Lens Flare**: Flare occurs when light enters the lens at an angle and bounces around inside, creating unwanted artifacts and reducing contrast. A lens hood minimizes this by shading the front of the lens.
- **Added Protection**: Besides improving image quality, lens hoods offer physical protection for the lens. They act as a barrier against bumps, drops, and even rain.
- **Enhanced Contrast**: By preventing stray light from hitting the front element, lens hoods help maintain rich color and contrast.

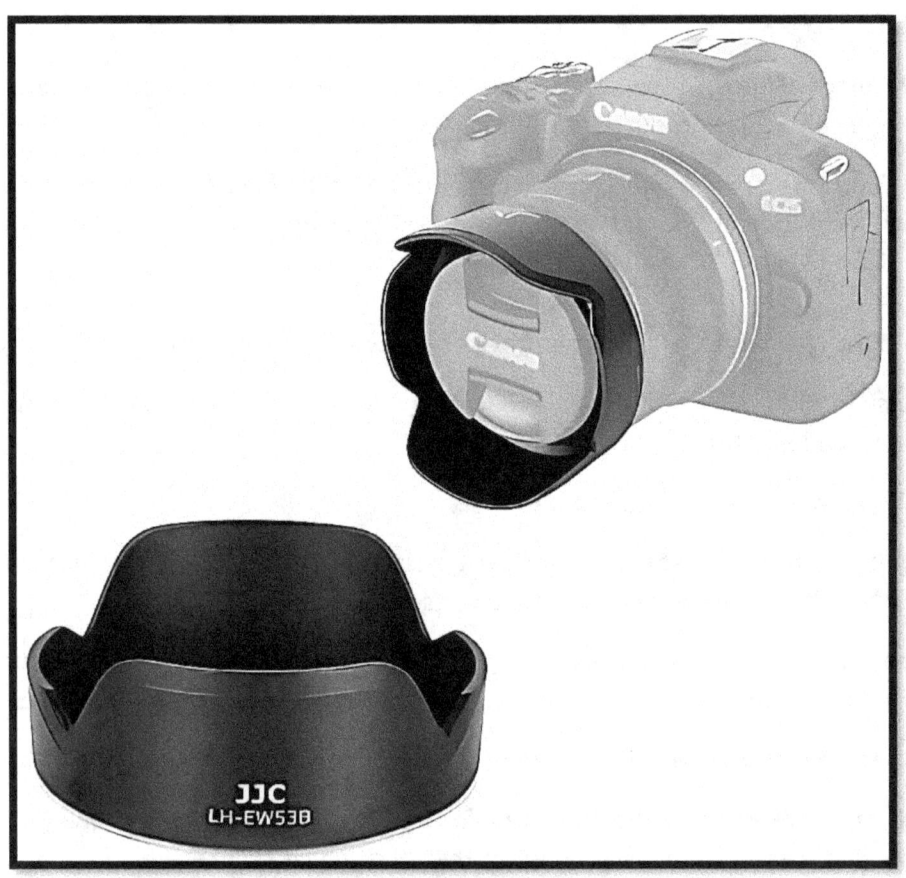

Lens Hoods

Types of Lens Hoods:

- **Petal-Shaped Hoods**: These hoods have cutouts that optimize the coverage for wide-angle lenses. The shape allows the hood to extend as far as possible without intruding into the image frame.

- **Round Hoods**: Common for telephoto and standard lenses, they provide more consistent shading around the lens and are simpler in design.

- **Built-In Hoods**: Found on some specialized lenses like macro lenses, these hoods are built into the body of the lens and extend or retract as needed.

How to Use a Lens Hood:

- **Attaching the Hood**: Align the hood's grooves with the bayonet mount on the lens and twist it clockwise until it locks in place.

- **Reversing for Storage**: Many hoods can be reversed and attached to the lens when not in use, making storage easier.

Practical Situations:

- **Outdoors in Bright Light**: A lens hood is invaluable when shooting outdoors to prevent flare from sunlight.
- **Indoor Photography**: Even under artificial light, stray reflections can impact your image. Using a lens hood can help control this.
- **Crowded Spaces**: In a busy environment, a lens hood can act as a buffer that protects your lens from accidental bumps or contact.

Advanced Insights for Professionals:

- **Custom Hoods for Tilt-Shift Lenses**: Professionals who use tilt-shift lenses for architectural photography may need specialized hoods or shading tools to avoid vignetting while maintaining image quality.
- **Creative Use of Flare**: Sometimes, lens flare can be used for artistic effects. Removing the hood and deliberately positioning a light source at an angle can create a warm, dreamy look.

3. Extenders: Extending Your Lens' Reach

Lens extenders, or teleconverters, are accessories that fit between the camera body and the lens, increasing the effective focal length. For example, a 1.4x extender will turn a 200mm lens into a 280mm lens. The Canon EOS R5 Mark II supports various extenders, expanding the capabilities of telephoto lenses without needing to purchase a longer lens.

Types of Extenders:

- **1.4x Extender**: Provides a 40% increase in focal length. Ideal for wildlife or sports photography where you need a bit more reach.
- **2x Extender**: Doubles the focal length, making a 200mm lens act as a 400mm lens. This is perfect for distant subjects but comes with some compromises.

Advantages of Using Extenders:

- **Cost-Effective**: Instead of purchasing a new, longer telephoto lens, using an extender is a more affordable way to increase reach.
- **Portability**: Extenders are much lighter and more compact than a large telephoto lens, making them ideal for travel.

Considerations When Using Extenders:

- **Reduced Maximum Aperture**: Using an extender will decrease the maximum aperture of your lens. For example, a 1.4x extender reduces the aperture by one stop (e.g., f/2.8 becomes f/4), while a 2x extender reduces it by two stops.
- **Potential Autofocus Limitations**: Some lenses may lose certain autofocus functions, especially in lower light conditions or with slower maximum apertures.
- **Image Quality Impact**: While high-quality extenders minimize image degradation, there can still be slight losses in sharpness and contrast. Using extenders from the same brand as your lens, such as Canon's own series, helps maintain quality.

Tips for Beginners:

- Start with a 1.4x extender to see how it affects your images. This smaller increase in focal length helps you adapt without significant compromises in performance.
- Ensure your lens is compatible with the extender. Not all lenses support teleconverters, and certain combinations may result in vignetting or AF issues.

Advanced Techniques for Professionals:

- **Combining with Stabilization**: The EOS R5 Mark II's in-body image stabilization (IBIS) works well with telephoto lenses and extenders, helping reduce shake when shooting handheld.
- **Manual Focus Adjustments**: When using a 2x extender in low-light or complex environments, switching to manual focus can help fine-tune sharpness.

Use Cases:

- **Wildlife Photography**: When photographing animals from a distance, an extender lets you get closer without disturbing your subject.
- **Sports Photography**: Extenders provide additional reach to capture distant action shots, like a player on a field or a race car on a track.
- **Astrophotography**: For celestial events, extenders can help frame the moon or planets more prominently, although careful focusing and stabilization are key.

Conclusion

Understanding and using filters, lens hoods, and extenders with your Canon EOS R5 Mark II can significantly enhance your photography. Filters provide creative control over light and exposure, lens hoods protect against unwanted glare and physical damage, and extenders allow you to expand your reach without additional heavy investment. Each accessory, whether used independently or combined, plays a critical role in helping both beginners and professionals capture sharper, more compelling images.

CHAPTER 6

SHOOTING STILL PHOTOGRAPHY

High-Resolution Image Capture and RAW Shooting

The Canon EOS R5 Mark II is renowned for its impressive image quality, thanks to its high-resolution sensor and the ability to shoot in RAW format. Understanding how to leverage these features can greatly enhance the quality of your photography, whether you're a beginner looking to improve or a professional aiming for perfection. This section explores the benefits of high-resolution image capture and RAW shooting, along with practical advice on how to use these features effectively.

1. What is High-Resolution Image Capture?

High-resolution image capture refers to taking photos at the highest possible pixel count that the camera can provide. The EOS R5 Mark II boasts a powerful full-frame sensor capable of capturing images at a resolution of up to 45 megapixels. This results in stunning detail and clarity, making it ideal for large prints, cropping without losing quality, and capturing intricate details in subjects like landscapes, portraits, and architecture.

Benefits of High-Resolution Capture:

- **Detailed Images**: A high pixel count ensures that even the finest textures and small elements in your scene are captured with clarity.

- **Large Print Potential**: High-resolution images are perfect for large-format printing without sacrificing image quality.

- **Flexible Cropping**: The large number of pixels allows you to crop photos and still maintain a high level of detail. This is useful in wildlife photography where you may not be able to get as close to your subject as desired.

Tips for Beginners:

- **Shooting at Maximum Resolution**: Always set your camera to the highest resolution for important shots. This ensures you capture maximum detail and gives you more flexibility in post-processing.

- **Memory Card Considerations**: High-resolution images take up more space, so invest in high-capacity, fast memory cards to handle the larger file sizes without slowing down your workflow.

Practical Example: When shooting a landscape scene, use the full 45-megapixel capability to capture every blade of grass and detail in the sky. This level of detail allows you to showcase the scene in all its grandeur or crop into specific sections without losing sharpness.

2. Understanding RAW Shooting

RAW is a file format that captures all image data recorded by the sensor. Unlike JPEGs, which compress and process the data, RAW files are uncompressed and unprocessed. This means you get a digital negative with maximum detail and flexibility for editing.

Benefits of Shooting in RAW:

- **Greater Editing Flexibility**: RAW files retain more information about color, brightness, and exposure. This allows you to adjust settings like white balance, exposure, and shadows without losing image quality.
- **Higher Dynamic Range**: RAW files capture more detail in the highlights and shadows. This is especially important for high-contrast scenes like sunsets or indoor photography with bright windows.
- **Non-Destructive Editing**: Adjustments to RAW files don't alter the original data. You can always revert to the untouched version, giving you peace of mind when experimenting in post-processing.

Tips for Beginners:

- **Start with RAW + JPEG**: If you're new to RAW shooting, try using the camera's "RAW + JPEG" setting. This will save a processed JPEG version along with the RAW file, giving you an instant shareable photo and an editable version for later.
- **Software for RAW Processing**: Use software like Adobe Lightroom, Canon's Digital Photo Professional (DPP), or Capture One to process RAW files. These programs are designed to take advantage of the rich data in RAW files, making edits smoother and more effective.

For Professionals: Shooting in RAW is a must for professional photographers who need the most control over their final images. Whether you're a portrait photographer fine-tuning skin tones or a landscape photographer balancing the brightness of a scene, RAW files provide the depth and flexibility required for professional-grade work.

3. Key Settings for High-Resolution and RAW Shooting

Resolution Settings:

- **Full Resolution**: Set your EOS R5 Mark II to its highest resolution in the image quality settings to ensure you capture all 45 megapixels.

- **C-RAW Format**: If storage space is a concern, consider using Canon's compressed RAW format (C-RAW). It offers smaller file sizes while maintaining most of the flexibility of standard RAW files.

RAW Settings:

- **RAW File Types**: The EOS R5 Mark II allows you to choose between standard RAW and C-RAW. Use standard RAW for maximum quality and C-RAW when you need to save space without significant quality loss.
- **Bit Depth**: The camera supports 14-bit RAW files, which store more color data and allow for smoother gradations, particularly useful in post-processing when adjusting tones and colors.

Tips for Optimal Shooting:

- **ISO Settings**: Lower ISO settings (e.g., ISO 100-400) help maintain image quality by reducing noise. The EOS R5 Mark II's sensor handles higher ISOs well, but sticking to lower settings ensures the cleanest files for high-resolution images.
- **Stability and Sharpness**: Use a tripod to minimize camera shake when shooting at high resolutions, especially in low-light conditions or when capturing detailed scenes like macro photography.

Practical Example: Imagine you are photographing a cityscape at twilight. By using RAW and setting the camera to its highest resolution, you can capture the subtle gradients in the sky and the details of building lights. This makes post-processing easier, allowing you to bring out shadow details and manage highlights without introducing noise or artifacts.

4. Challenges of High-Resolution and RAW Shooting

Large File Sizes: High-resolution images and RAW files take up significant storage space. Each 45-megapixel RAW file can be over 50 MB, depending on the scene. To handle this, invest in high-capacity memory cards (at least 128 GB or higher) and use UHS-II cards for faster write speeds.

Slower Continuous Shooting: Although the EOS R5 Mark II supports high-speed continuous shooting, using the highest resolution and RAW format can slow the buffer rate. This is important to consider during action or wildlife photography.

Post-Processing Demands: RAW files require more post-processing effort than JPEGs. This involves time and a learning curve if you're not familiar with editing software.

Solutions:

- **Workflow Optimization**: Develop a routine in software like Adobe Lightroom, using batch processing for basic adjustments such as exposure and white balance.
- **Use of C-RAW**: When balancing quality and file size, C-RAW is a helpful middle ground.
- **External Storage**: Utilize external hard drives or cloud storage solutions to manage and back up your images efficiently.

5. Workflow Tips for High-Resolution and RAW Images

Importing and Organizing:

- **Importing**: Use software that can handle RAW files efficiently. Import photos into a structured folder system to keep track of your high-resolution files.
- **Backup Strategy**: Always have a backup copy of your RAW files, either on an external drive or a cloud service, to protect against data loss.

Editing Process:

- **Initial Adjustments**: Start with exposure correction and white balance. RAW files maintain more data, so you can adjust these without degrading image quality.
- **Sharpening and Noise Reduction**: High-resolution images can show more detail but also more noise, especially in shadows. Apply noise reduction selectively and sharpen to enhance detail without making the image look artificial.
- **Export Settings**: Export images at the necessary resolution for your intended use, whether that's web sharing (compressed and resized) or large prints (high resolution).

For Professionals: Consider using a dual-card setup on the EOS R5 Mark II. Record RAW files to a high-speed CFexpress card for primary use and JPEGs to an SD card for quick review and client previews.

Advanced Tip:

- **Focus Stacking**: For macro or landscape photographers, shoot a series of high-resolution images at different focus points and merge them in post-processing software. This maximizes depth of field and ensures the entire scene is sharp.

Conclusion

Shooting high-resolution images and working with RAW files on the Canon EOS R5 Mark II can dramatically improve the quality and flexibility of your photography. High-resolution capture ensures every detail is preserved, while RAW shooting provides the maximum potential for post-processing. While the larger file sizes and need for more advanced editing may present challenges, the benefits far outweigh these considerations, especially for those seeking professional-level results. By following these tips and techniques, you can master the art of high-resolution photography and make the most of your Canon EOS R5 Mark II.

Burst Shooting and High-Speed Photography

The Canon EOS R5 Mark II is equipped with powerful features for burst shooting and high-speed photography, making it a top choice for capturing fast-paced action. Whether you're a beginner learning the ropes or a professional shooting high-stakes events, understanding how to utilize these features effectively can transform your photography. In this section, we'll break down what burst shooting and high-speed photography are, why they matter, and how to get the best results with your Canon EOS R5 Mark II.

1. What is Burst Shooting and Why Use It?

Burst shooting, also known as continuous shooting, involves capturing a series of images in quick succession with a single press of the shutter button. This is essential for action photography where precise timing can make the difference between an average shot and an exceptional one.

When to Use Burst Shooting:

- **Sports and Action**: Perfect for capturing the peak of motion, like a soccer player striking the ball or a gymnast in mid-air.
- **Wildlife**: Useful for photographing animals in motion, such as birds taking flight or a cheetah sprinting.
- **Candid Moments**: Burst shooting can help you capture fleeting expressions or interactions during events like weddings.

Benefits of Burst Shooting:

- **Multiple Options**: Shooting continuously increases the chance of capturing the perfect moment.
- **Motion Analysis**: By having a series of images, you can review the sequence to better understand motion, which is helpful for both learning and improving timing in your photography.

Key Terms to Understand:

- **Frames Per Second (FPS)**: The number of images the camera can take per second during burst shooting. The Canon EOS R5 Mark II can achieve up to 12 FPS with its mechanical shutter and up to 20 FPS with its electronic shutter.

- **Buffer**: The camera's internal memory that temporarily holds images before they are written to the memory card. A larger buffer allows for longer bursts without slowing down.

2. How to Set Up Burst Shooting on the Canon EOS R5 Mark II

To use burst shooting effectively, you need to set up the camera properly. Here's how:

Step-by-Step Guide:

- **Navigate to the Shooting Mode**: Press the "Drive" button or go to the camera's main menu and select "Drive Mode."
- **Choose the Continuous Shooting Option**: Select either "High-Speed Continuous" (H+) for maximum FPS or "Low-Speed Continuous" (H) for a more controlled burst.
- **Adjust Settings Based on Your Needs**:
    - **Mechanical vs. Electronic Shutter**: The mechanical shutter provides a traditional feel and eliminates potential rolling shutter effects in fast-moving subjects. The electronic shutter is silent and enables the maximum FPS, which is ideal for wildlife photography where quiet operation is essential.
    - **Buffer Considerations**: If you're shooting in RAW, the buffer will fill faster than when shooting in JPEG. Use high-speed CFexpress cards to help clear the buffer quickly and maintain continuous shooting.

Tips for Beginners:

- **Start with JPEG**: While learning, set the camera to shoot in high-quality JPEG. This allows for longer burst durations since JPEG files are smaller than RAW.
- **Use AF Tracking**: Activate AI Servo AF mode to continuously focus on moving subjects while shooting in bursts.

Advanced Settings for Professionals:

- **Customizing FPS**: You can customize the FPS setting in the menu to balance speed and buffer performance, depending on the situation.
- **Back-Button Focus**: Assigning autofocus to a back button (e.g., AF-ON) allows you to focus separately from the shutter release, ensuring the camera maintains focus as you shoot in bursts.

3. Mastering High-Speed Photography

High-speed photography is about freezing moments that happen so quickly they are often missed by the naked eye. The EOS R5 Mark II's advanced shutter system and fast processing power make it ideal for capturing these split-second actions.

Situations Perfect for High-Speed Photography:

- **Splash Photography**: Capturing the precise moment a drop of water hits a surface.
- **Sports**: Freezing the motion of an athlete in action.
- **Wildlife**: Documenting a bird's wings mid-flap or a predator leaping to catch prey.

Techniques for High-Speed Success:

- **Fast Shutter Speeds**: Use shutter speeds of at least 1/1000s or higher to freeze motion. For extremely fast subjects like hummingbird wings, 1/4000s or faster may be required.
- **Adequate Lighting**: High shutter speeds reduce the amount of light reaching the sensor. Ensure you have ample light, whether through natural sources or external flashes.
- **Burst Mode and Continuous AF**: Combine burst shooting with continuous autofocus to track moving subjects and capture them sharply across multiple frames.

Practical Example: Imagine photographing a skateboarder performing a trick. Set the camera to "High-Speed Continuous" mode with a shutter speed of 1/2000s. Keep the focus on AI Servo AF to track the skater, and hold the shutter button as they perform the move. The burst mode ensures you capture each part of the trick, and the fast shutter freezes their motion crisply.

4. Enhancing Burst Shooting with Autofocus and Tracking

The Canon EOS R5 Mark II's Dual Pixel CMOS AF II system is a game-changer for high-speed photography. It provides rapid and accurate autofocus across nearly the entire frame, making it easier to track fast-moving subjects.

AF Tracking Features:

- **Subject Detection**: The camera can detect and track human eyes, animals, and even vehicles. This helps maintain focus even when subjects move unpredictably.
- **Custom AF Settings**: The R5 Mark II allows users to fine-tune AF sensitivity and tracking speed to match the pace of their subject. For instance, you can set the AF to be more responsive for sudden subject changes or slower for smoother transitions.

Tips for Beginners:

- **Use Face and Eye Detection**: Enable this feature for portraits or events to keep the subject's face in sharp focus, even when moving.
- **Zone AF**: For tracking larger moving subjects, use Zone AF. This allows the camera to use multiple focus points for better tracking performance.

Advanced Tips for Professionals:

- **Custom AF Cases**: The EOS R5 Mark II has customizable AF cases designed for different scenarios, like erratic motion or subjects that accelerate/decelerate suddenly. Experiment with these to find the optimal setting for your specific needs.
- **Lens Choice**: Pair the camera with lenses that have fast autofocus motors (e.g., Canon RF lenses) for the best results.

5. Managing Buffer and Memory Cards

High-speed and burst shooting generate a lot of data. Ensuring your memory cards can keep up with the camera's write speed is essential for continuous shooting without interruptions.

Choosing the Right Memory Cards:

- **CFexpress Cards**: These cards have higher write speeds compared to traditional SD cards, allowing the buffer to clear faster. This is critical when shooting RAW in high-speed bursts.
- **UHS-II SD Cards**: If using an SD card, opt for UHS-II, which supports faster data transfer than UHS-I.

Buffer Management Tips:

- **Shoot in C-RAW**: Compressed RAW files are smaller and allow longer continuous bursts before filling the buffer.
- **Monitor Buffer Status**: The viewfinder or LCD screen shows the remaining buffer capacity. Keep an eye on it, especially during long bursts, to avoid missing critical moments.

Example: If you're photographing a fast-paced soccer match, use a high-capacity CFexpress card and monitor the buffer indicator. Switch to JPEG or C-RAW if you notice the buffer filling quickly, ensuring you capture the entire game without delays.

6. Analyzing and Improving High-Speed Shooting

After capturing images using burst shooting or high-speed techniques, reviewing and analyzing the shots can help refine your approach:

Reviewing Shots:

- **Use the Burst Playback Feature**: The EOS R5 Mark II allows you to review burst shots in a series. This makes it easy to compare frames and select the best one.
- **Check Focus and Sharpness**: Zoom in to ensure the subject is sharply in focus, especially when tracking moving subjects.

Post-Processing Considerations:

- **Select the Best Frames**: For action sequences, choose the frame that best captures the moment you want to highlight.
- **Noise Reduction**: High-speed photography may sometimes require higher ISO settings. Use post-processing software to reduce noise while maintaining detail.
- **Color and Exposure Corrections**: Adjust the exposure, shadows, and highlights, particularly for sports and wildlife photos taken in dynamic lighting conditions.

Conclusion

Burst shooting and high-speed photography are powerful tools for capturing dynamic and fleeting moments with the Canon EOS R5 Mark II. By mastering the camera's settings, understanding how to manage autofocus and tracking, and selecting the right memory cards, photographers can achieve exceptional results in challenging scenarios. Whether you're a beginner exploring action shots or a seasoned professional fine-tuning your sports photography, the techniques and tips in this section will ensure you make the most of your camera's capabilities.

Creative Shooting: HDR, Multiple Exposure, and Bracketing

The Canon EOS R5 Mark II is not just designed for standard photography; it also offers creative features that can elevate your images. Understanding how to use HDR (High Dynamic Range), multiple exposure, and bracketing modes will empower you to experiment and capture stunning, unique photos. This section explores these techniques, explaining each concept, their benefits, and step-by-step instructions on how to use them effectively.

1. HDR (High Dynamic Range) Photography

HDR photography involves capturing and combining multiple images taken at different exposures to create a single photo with a greater dynamic range. This results in more detail in both the brightest and darkest areas of the image.

Why Use HDR?

- **Balanced Exposure**: HDR is ideal for high-contrast scenes, such as landscapes with a bright sky and shadowed foreground, or interiors with windows showing the outside.

- **Enhanced Details**: Combining exposures allows you to preserve details that would otherwise be lost in a single exposure.

How HDR Works: The Canon EOS R5 Mark II captures multiple photos at varying exposure levels and then merges them automatically or lets you process them manually in post-production.

Setting Up HDR on the EOS R5 Mark II:

- **Navigate to HDR Mode**: Access the HDR mode through the camera's menu under "Shooting Settings."

- **Select HDR Options**:
    - **Auto Align**: Ensures the images align correctly, useful for handheld shots.
    - **Exposure Level**: Choose the range of exposure differences between shots (e.g., ±1 EV, ±2 EV).

- **Select Merge Option**: You can opt to have the camera automatically merge the images or save them individually for post-processing.

Tips for Beginners:

- **Use a Tripod**: While the camera's auto-align feature is useful, using a tripod can help ensure your images align perfectly, especially for complex scenes.

- **Start with Built-in HDR**: Let the camera combine the images automatically to get a feel for the results before moving on to manual HDR processing.

Advanced Tips for Professionals:

- **Manual HDR Merging**: Capture the images in RAW and use software like Adobe Photoshop or Lightroom to blend them manually. This allows for more control over the final look, letting you adjust how much detail is revealed in highlights and shadows.

- **Avoid Overprocessing**: Keep the HDR effect natural to avoid overly surreal or unrealistic images unless that's the artistic style you're pursuing.

2. Multiple Exposure Photography

Multiple exposure involves combining two or more images into a single frame. This technique can be used to create artistic effects, tell stories, or add creative elements to a photo.

Why Use Multiple Exposure?

- **Creative Expression**: This technique opens up opportunities for creative storytelling by combining different elements, such as a portrait overlaid with a landscape.

- **Artistic Effects**: Achieve ethereal or surreal effects that aren't possible with standard photography.

How to Use Multiple Exposure on the EOS R5 Mark II:

- **Navigate to Multiple Exposure Mode**: Select "Multiple Exposure" from the "Shooting Settings" menu.
- **Choose the Number of Exposures**: You can set how many images you want to combine (usually 2-9).
- **Select the Blending Mode**:
    - **Additive**: Simple merging of images, ideal for enhancing brightness.
    - **Average**: Balances the exposure across all combined images.
    - **Bright/Dark**: Prioritizes either the brighter or darker parts of the images to create interesting effects.
- **Capture Your Base Image**: This can be an existing photo or a new shot.
- **Capture Additional Images**: Shoot the remaining exposures while using the camera's live preview to see how each added image affects the final result.

Practical Example: Try a double exposure by shooting a portrait as your base image and overlaying it with a nature scene like trees or flowers. The final combined image can depict a connection between the subject and their environment.

Tips for Beginners:

- **Plan Your Shots**: Visualize how the combined images will interact. Start with simple combinations, such as silhouettes and textured backgrounds.
- **Use Live View**: The EOS R5 Mark II's live view helps you see how the images blend, making adjustments easier before you commit to a final shot.

Advanced Techniques for Professionals:

- **Experiment with Transparency**: Adjusting the opacity of each exposure gives you more control over how the images merge.
- **Layered Storytelling**: Combine images that tell a narrative or evoke an emotional response, such as overlaying a cityscape with a silhouette of a traveler to imply exploration.

3. Bracketing for Precision

Bracketing is a technique where the camera captures multiple shots of the same scene at different exposure levels. This method ensures you have a well-exposed image and is also the foundation for creating HDR photos.

Why Use Bracketing?

- **Perfect Exposure**: Bracketing helps ensure that at least one image in the sequence is properly exposed, which is crucial for tricky lighting conditions.
- **HDR Base**: The individual images from bracketing can be combined later to create an HDR image with more control over tone mapping.

How to Set Up Exposure Bracketing:

- **Navigate to Bracketing Settings**: Access this through the camera's "Shooting Menu" under "Exposure Comp./AEB (Auto Exposure Bracketing)."
- **Set the Bracketing Range**: Choose how many stops above and below the standard exposure the camera will shoot (e.g., ±1, ±2, or ±3 EV).
- **Select the Number of Shots**: The EOS R5 Mark II can take 3, 5, or even more bracketed shots, depending on the exposure range set.
- **Use Continuous Shooting Mode**: This helps capture the bracketed shots quickly to minimize changes in the scene between exposures.

Tips for Beginners:

- **Start with a ±1 EV Bracket**: This range is a safe starting point for most scenes with moderate contrast.
- **Use Auto ISO**: In some cases, setting ISO to auto can help maintain consistent exposure settings across bracketed shots.

For Professionals:

- **Advanced Bracketing**: Use bracketing combined with manual adjustments to create a broader range of exposures for post-processing. This is especially useful for scenes with complex lighting, such as sunsets.
- **Remote Shutter Release**: To minimize camera shake, use a remote trigger or the camera's self-timer to take bracketed shots, especially when a tripod is in use.

Practical Use Case: Imagine photographing a scene with a bright sky and a dark foreground. Using a 5-shot bracket with exposures at -2, -1, 0, +1, and +2 EV ensures that you capture the details in both the sky and the foreground. Later, you can blend these exposures to create a balanced image with rich detail across all tonal ranges.

4. Combining Techniques for Greater Creativity

The Canon EOS R5 Mark II allows you to combine these features to push your photography further. For example, you can use bracketing to create base images for HDR while incorporating multiple exposure techniques for added artistic flair.

Practical Workflow:

- **Shoot with Bracketing**: Capture a set of images at different exposures.
- **Merge for HDR**: Use software to merge these images into an HDR photo.
- **Overlay for Multiple Exposure**: Blend a portrait or other image with the HDR base for a creative composite.

Tips for Success:

- **Experiment with Blending**: Use different blend modes and exposures in multiple exposure photography to see how they interact with HDR backgrounds.
- **Plan Your Scenes**: Think ahead about which scenes would benefit from the combined use of HDR and multiple exposures for dramatic, detailed, and layered results.

Conclusion

Creative shooting with the Canon EOS R5 Mark II goes beyond traditional photography. Using HDR, multiple exposure, and bracketing, you can capture stunningly detailed images, craft unique compositions, and handle challenging lighting conditions with ease. For beginners, these features provide a gateway to more artistic photography, while professionals can use them to expand their creative toolkit and tell more compelling stories. Mastering these techniques will enhance your photography and set your work apart from standard shots.

CHAPTER 7

VIDEO RECORDING CAPABILITIES

8K and 4K Video Recording Options on the Canon EOS R5 Mark II

Canon's EOS R5 Mark II is renowned for its high-resolution video capabilities, which set a new standard in the world of mirrorless cameras. With support for both 8K and 4K video recording, the camera delivers cinematic-quality video in two powerful resolutions. In this section, we'll go over the fundamentals of 8K and 4K recording, explore the differences and advantages of each, and explain how to choose and set up the right options for your specific shooting needs.

Understanding 8K and 4K Resolution

In simple terms, the resolution of a video refers to the number of pixels that make up the image. Higher resolutions mean more pixels, which allows for more detail, clarity, and sharpness.

- **8K Video Resolution**: 8K resolution provides an ultra-high-definition image with a pixel count of approximately 7680 x 4320 pixels. That's about 33 million pixels, which is four times the resolution of 4K and sixteen times that of Full HD (1080p). The 8K resolution is ideal for scenarios that require extreme detail, such as professional film projects, landscape cinematography, and productions intended for large screen displays. Additionally, 8K allows flexibility in post-production, where you can crop or zoom without losing image quality.

- **4K Video Resolution**: 4K video has a pixel count of about 3840 x 2160 pixels. While it's half the resolution of 8K, it still offers stunning clarity, and is widely used in television, web content, and many professional video projects. 4K is also more manageable than 8K in terms of storage and processing power, making it an excellent option for users who want high-quality results without the challenges associated with 8K files.

Benefits of 8K and 4K Recording on the EOS R5 Mark II

The Canon EOS R5 Mark II's video capabilities aren't just about high resolutions; they include practical benefits that make filming easier and more flexible.

- **Enhanced Detail and Clarity**: With more pixels, both 8K and 4K resolutions capture extremely fine details, allowing for sharp, vivid footage even when viewed on large screens.

- **Flexibility in Post-Production**: Higher resolutions make it possible to crop, stabilize, or zoom in on footage without significantly losing quality, which can be crucial for reframing shots or adding motion effects.

- **Professional Quality and Compatibility**: 4K is now the industry standard for broadcast and online content, while 8K positions you for future-proofing your projects as displays continue to improve and 8K becomes more widely accessible.

Key Considerations for 8K and 4K Recording

While the benefits of high-resolution video are clear, understanding the requirements and potential challenges of 8K and 4K recording is essential for making the most of these capabilities.

- **Storage Space**: Both 8K and 4K video files require a significant amount of storage due to the amount of data captured in each frame. A single minute of 8K video, for example, can easily exceed a gigabyte in size depending on the compression format, while 4K is more manageable but still large. The Canon EOS R5 Mark II supports high-capacity CFexpress cards and SD cards, which are essential for these large files.

- **Processing Power**: Editing high-resolution video demands more from your computer's processor, RAM, and storage. Working with 8K footage requires a particularly powerful setup, as it involves handling massive amounts of data.

- **Battery Usage**: Recording in high resolutions, especially at higher frame rates, uses more processing power and battery life. For extended 8K or 4K shooting sessions, it's advisable to carry extra batteries or use an external power source.

- **Overheating**: High-resolution recording generates a lot of heat. While the Canon EOS R5 Mark II has improved cooling mechanisms, users may still encounter heat limitations when recording in 8K or 4K for extended periods, especially in warmer environments. Shooting in intervals and using external fans can help manage overheating.

8K Recording Options on the Canon EOS R5 Mark II

The Canon EOS R5 Mark II offers flexible 8K recording modes, allowing users to choose the option that best suits their project and available resources.

- **8K DCI (Digital Cinema Initiatives)**: This setting uses the full sensor and captures in 8K resolution for a cinematic look with an aspect ratio of 17:9, which is preferred in professional filmmaking. It provides the highest quality possible and maximizes the sensor's capabilities.

- **8K UHD (Ultra High Definition)**: 8K UHD has a 16:9 aspect ratio, which is the standard for television and internet content. This option is ideal if you're planning to publish the video on YouTube or similar platforms.

- **8K RAW**: In addition to standard compressed formats, the R5 Mark II allows 8K RAW recording, which captures uncompressed data directly from the sensor. RAW format gives the most flexibility in post-production, allowing for adjustments to color, exposure, and other settings without quality loss. However, it generates very large files and requires powerful editing software and hardware.

4K Recording Options on the Canon EOS R5 Mark II

While 8K is groundbreaking, 4K remains the go-to resolution for many users. The EOS R5 Mark II offers a variety of 4K modes tailored for different needs.

- **4K DCI and UHD**: Like 8K, 4K on the EOS R5 Mark II can be recorded in DCI (17:9 aspect ratio) or UHD (16:9 aspect ratio) resolutions. 4K DCI is often chosen for film production, while 4K UHD is a better fit for broadcast and online media.

- **4K HQ (High Quality)**: This mode down-samples the 8K sensor data into a 4K file, resulting in even sharper and cleaner footage than standard 4K. 4K HQ is particularly beneficial for high-end projects where visual fidelity is paramount.

- **4K 120fps (High Frame Rate)**: The Canon EOS R5 Mark II can capture 4K video at up to 120 frames per second (fps), allowing for smooth, detailed slow-motion effects. High frame rates are excellent for action scenes, wildlife, sports, and creative projects that require a slow-motion aesthetic. Note that shooting at 120fps requires more storage and can generate extra heat.

Choosing the Right Resolution for Your Project

Selecting the ideal resolution for a project involves balancing quality needs with practical limitations such as storage, battery life, and editing capabilities.

- **For Beginners**: If you're new to video recording, start with 4K UHD or 4K HQ for an excellent balance of quality and manageability. 4K resolutions are easier to handle on most computers and provide fantastic visual results without overwhelming file sizes or overheating issues.

- **For Professionals**: Experienced videographers and professionals working on high-budget projects may benefit from 8K, particularly if the project involves large-screen viewing or needs the flexibility of cropping in post-production. However, 4K HQ and 4K 120fps are also excellent options for high-quality footage in manageable file sizes.

Setting Up 8K and 4K Video Recording on the EOS R5 Mark II

Here's how to set up your Canon EOS R5 Mark II for 8K or 4K recording:

- **Open the Video Settings Menu**: In the main menu, go to "Shoot" settings, then select "Movie Rec Quality" to access the resolution options.

- **Select Resolution and Frame Rate**: Choose between 8K DCI, 8K UHD, 4K DCI, or 4K UHD, and select your preferred frame rate. Remember that higher frame rates create smoother motion but use more storage.

- **Adjust Compression Format**: Select RAW for maximum quality and post-production flexibility, or choose a compressed format if you're aiming for smaller file sizes.

- **Set Up Audio and Stabilization**: Ensure that audio settings are properly configured for external or internal microphones, and enable In-Body Image Stabilization (IBIS) if needed, especially for handheld shots.

Conclusion

By understanding the Canon EOS R5 Mark II's 8K and 4K video options, you can unlock the full potential of this camera, capturing cinematic quality that enhances any project. Whether you're a beginner exploring 4K for the first time or a seasoned professional working with 8K, these features provide a range of creative possibilities that meet the needs of virtually any production.

Frame Rates, Resolutions, and Formats on the Canon EOS R5 Mark II

The Canon EOS R5 Mark II offers a wide range of frame rates, resolutions, and formats for video recording, allowing both beginners and professionals to capture footage in high quality, adaptable to different kinds of projects. This section explains what each of these terms means, how they impact your video recordings, and how to choose the right settings based on your project goals.

Understanding Frame Rates

Frame rate is the number of individual frames (or images) captured per second in a video. It is measured in frames per second (fps), with common frame rates being 24fps, 30fps, and 60fps. The frame rate you choose affects the look and feel of your video, with each frame rate serving different purposes and styles of video.

- **24fps (Frames Per Second)**: This frame rate is commonly used in filmmaking and gives footage a cinematic quality. It's often preferred for narrative work like movies or short films because of its natural, slightly motion-blurred look. 24fps is ideal if you want your video to have a classic film aesthetic.

- **30fps**: This frame rate is often used for television and online videos, providing a slightly smoother look than 24fps while still maintaining a "realistic" feel. It's a good choice for tutorials, interviews, and content that will be uploaded to social media or video platforms like YouTube.

- **60fps**: This frame rate provides even smoother motion and is great for capturing fast-moving subjects, such as in sports, wildlife, or action scenes. It's also commonly used if you plan to create slow-motion effects in post-production, as slowing down 60fps footage results in a smooth slow-motion video when played at lower speeds.

- **120fps**: The EOS R5 Mark II also supports 120fps at 4K resolution, which is excellent for achieving very slow-motion effects, allowing for dramatic capture of fast-moving scenes. This is a great option for creative projects that need ultra-smooth slow-motion sequences, such as extreme sports or artistic effects.

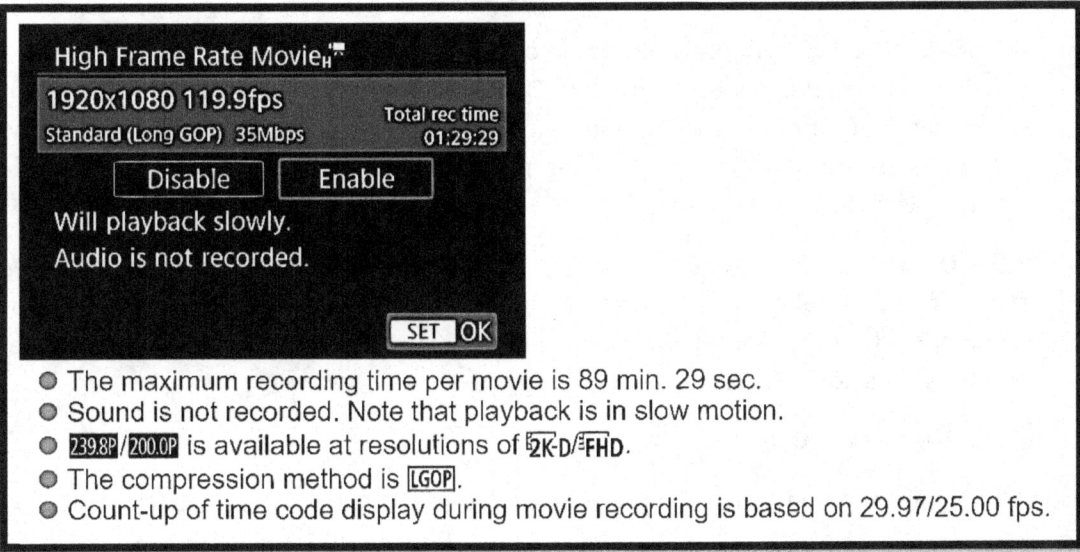

Choosing the Right Frame Rate

The choice of frame rate often depends on the style of video you are producing:

- **Cinematic Style**: Use 24fps for a movie-like feel.

- **Realistic or Documentary Style**: 30fps gives a natural look with smooth motion.

- **Slow Motion**: 60fps or 120fps allow for crisp slow-motion effects in post-production.

Higher frame rates capture more motion data, but they require more storage and processing power. It's also important to note that higher frame rates may use more battery and can increase the risk of the camera overheating during long recording sessions.

Understanding Video Resolution

Resolution refers to the number of pixels that make up each frame in your video, which impacts the clarity and detail. On the Canon EOS R5 Mark II, you have access to several resolutions, including 8K, 4K, and Full HD (1080p), each with its own strengths and purposes.

- **8K (7680 x 4320 pixels):** This is the highest resolution available on the EOS R5 Mark II, providing extreme detail with about 33 million pixels per frame. 8K is ideal for professional projects that need maximum clarity and fine detail. It's great for large-screen displays, high-end productions, or any situation where you may need to crop or zoom in post-production without losing quality. However, 8K files are very large and require substantial storage space and processing power.

- **4K (3840 x 2160 pixels):** 4K is a popular choice for most high-definition video work and offers four times the resolution of Full HD. It provides excellent clarity while being more manageable in terms of file size and editing requirements than 8K. 4K is ideal for web content, professional videos, and online platforms like YouTube, where it's the highest standard viewers typically expect.

- **Full HD 1080p (1920 x 1080 pixels):** Full HD is still widely used for online content and streaming, especially on platforms where 4K isn't necessary or practical. It's also an efficient choice when storage space is limited, or if you need a format that can be easily edited on less powerful computers.

Choosing the Right Resolution

Choosing the right resolution depends on your project requirements, storage capacity, and editing setup:

- **High-End and Professional Projects:** 8K offers the highest quality and flexibility in post-production but requires a powerful computer and large storage capacity.

- **High-Quality Online Content:** 4K strikes a good balance of quality and file size and is suitable for most online content.

- **Everyday or Casual Projects:** 1080p is great for social media, live streaming, or projects where file size and ease of editing are priorities.

Video Formats on the EOS R5 Mark II

Video format refers to how the camera encodes and compresses the video file. Different formats are used based on the quality needs and intended workflow for the video footage. The Canon EOS R5 Mark II provides several options for recording format, including MP4 and RAW, each suitable for different types of projects.

- **MP4 (H.264/H.265)**: The MP4 format uses the H.264 or H.265 compression standards, which balance quality and file size efficiently. H.264 is widely compatible with editing software and devices, while H.265 offers better compression, reducing file size without losing quality. MP4 is ideal for everyday recording, online video sharing, and projects that don't require extensive post-production editing.

- **RAW (Cinema RAW Light)**: RAW format captures uncompressed video data, preserving as much detail and color information as possible. This format is ideal for professional filmmakers and videographers who want full control over color grading, exposure adjustments, and other elements in post-production. RAW files are large and require more storage and processing power, but they offer the greatest flexibility for high-end editing.

- **ALL-I (Intra-frame Compression)**: This format compresses each frame independently, making it easier to edit and providing high image quality, especially for fast-moving scenes. ALL-I format files are larger but are often preferred by editors for projects where each frame's detail matters, such as action or sports footage.

- **IPB (Inter-frame Compression)**: IPB compresses frames based on changes between them, resulting in smaller files but potentially less detail for fast-moving objects. It's efficient and produces smaller file sizes, making it ideal for longer recording sessions, casual projects, or where storage is limited.

Setting Up Frame Rates, Resolutions, and Formats on the Canon EOS R5 Mark II

The Canon EOS R5 Mark II's settings menu makes it easy to select your desired frame rate, resolution, and format. Here's a step-by-step guide to setting up each of these options on your camera.

- **Access the Video Menu**: Turn the mode dial to "Movie" mode to enter video recording mode. Press the "Menu" button to access the settings.

- **Choose Your Resolution**: In the "Movie Rec Quality" menu, select the desired resolution (8K, 4K, or 1080p). Keep in mind that higher resolutions use more storage space.

- **Set the Frame Rate**: In the same menu, select your preferred frame rate based on your project needs (24fps, 30fps, 60fps, or 120fps). Remember, higher frame rates offer smoother motion but increase storage requirements.

- **Select the Video Format**: Choose between MP4, RAW, ALL-I, or IPB based on your editing and storage needs. If you're aiming for maximum editing flexibility, RAW or ALL-I formats are ideal; if storage space is a priority, IPB is a better choice.

- **Verify Your Settings**: Once you've selected your frame rate, resolution, and format, review your settings and make any final adjustments. Consider testing a short recording to ensure the setup meets your expectations.

Practical Tips for Managing Frame Rates, Resolutions, and Formats

- **Plan for Storage**: Higher resolutions and frame rates consume more storage, so use high-capacity SD or CFexpress cards to avoid running out of space during a shoot.

- **Check Compatibility**: If you're using RAW or high-frame-rate formats, make sure your editing software and computer can handle the file sizes and processing requirements.

- **Balance Quality and Practicality**: While 8K and high frame rates provide superior quality, they may not be necessary for every project. Consider the needs of your final product when choosing settings.

- **Practice with Different Settings**: Familiarizing yourself with various frame rates, resolutions, and formats will help you gain confidence in selecting the best setup for each project.

Conclusion

By mastering frame rates, resolutions, and formats on the Canon EOS R5 Mark II, you can produce videos that match your creative vision, whether you're working on a high-end project or a quick online video.

Audio Settings and External Microphone Use on the Canon EOS R5 Mark II

Audio quality is an essential part of any video project. While the Canon EOS R5 Mark II is well-known for its video capabilities, it also provides a range of audio options to capture high-quality sound. In this section, we'll break down the audio settings available on the R5 Mark II, how to get the most from the camera's built-in microphone, and how to achieve professional sound quality using external microphones. This setup will help you record clear and crisp audio for a variety of shooting environments.

Understanding Audio Settings on the EOS R5 Mark II

The audio settings on the Canon EOS R5 Mark II allow you to control how sound is recorded. Whether you're using the built-in microphone or an external microphone, setting up your audio properly is essential for clear, professional-sounding results.

1. **Audio Levels (Gain Control)**: Audio levels, or gain, refer to the sensitivity of the microphone to the sounds around it. The R5 Mark II allows you to adjust audio levels manually or automatically, helping to balance sound without distortion or clipping.

2. **Automatic vs. Manual Audio Control**: In **Automatic Audio Control**, the camera adjusts the audio levels based on the volume of sounds in the environment. This is useful in unpredictable audio environments, such as a crowded street or noisy event. **Manual Audio Control** allows you to set audio levels precisely, which is ideal for consistent sound recording, such as interviews or studio settings where you have control over noise levels.

3. **Wind Noise Reduction**: If you're recording outdoors, wind noise can be a problem. The EOS R5 Mark II includes a wind noise reduction option that reduces low-frequency noise caused by wind, making audio clearer. However, this feature is mainly effective with the built-in microphone; for high-quality external microphones, it's often better to use a dedicated windscreen or "deadcat" cover.

4. **Sound Recording Level Meter**: The Canon EOS R5 Mark II has an on-screen sound level meter, which is a visual guide to help you monitor the audio levels in real-time. It's essential to keep an eye on this meter while recording, ensuring that levels don't reach the red zone, which indicates clipping and potential distortion.

Setting Up Audio on the EOS R5 Mark II

To access the audio settings on your R5 Mark II:

- **Enter the Menu**: Press the "Menu" button, navigate to the audio settings in the video recording settings, and select "Sound Recording."

- **Choose Automatic or Manual**: In the Sound Recording menu, select either Automatic or Manual audio control. For Manual, use the control dial to increase or decrease audio levels.

- **Activate Wind Noise Reduction**: In the same menu, activate "Wind Filter" if you're recording outdoors and using the built-in microphone.

- **Monitor Levels Using the Sound Meter**: As you adjust settings, check the sound recording level meter on the screen. Aim to keep levels within the safe range (usually around -12dB to -6dB) to avoid distortion.

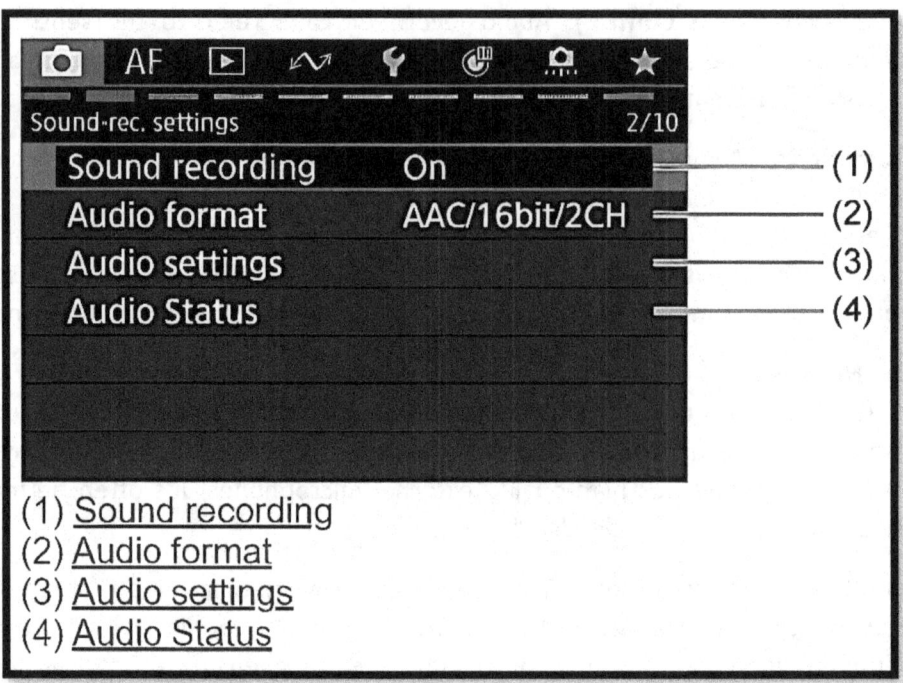

(1) Sound recording
(2) Audio format
(3) Audio settings
(4) Audio Status

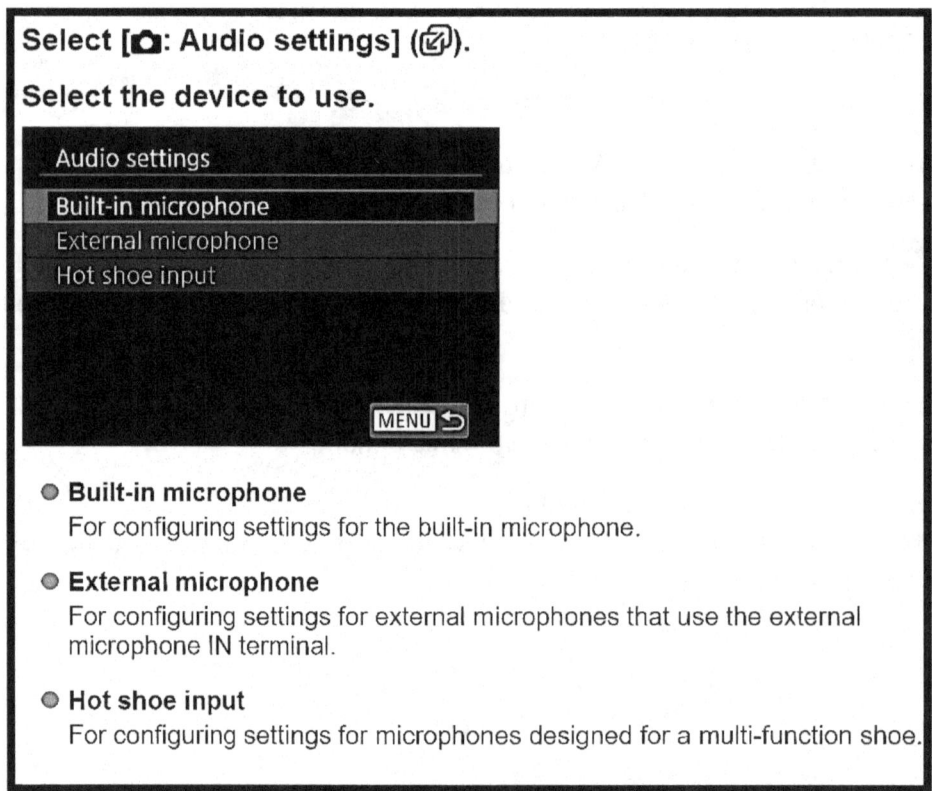

Set the item.

When set to [Built-in microphone]

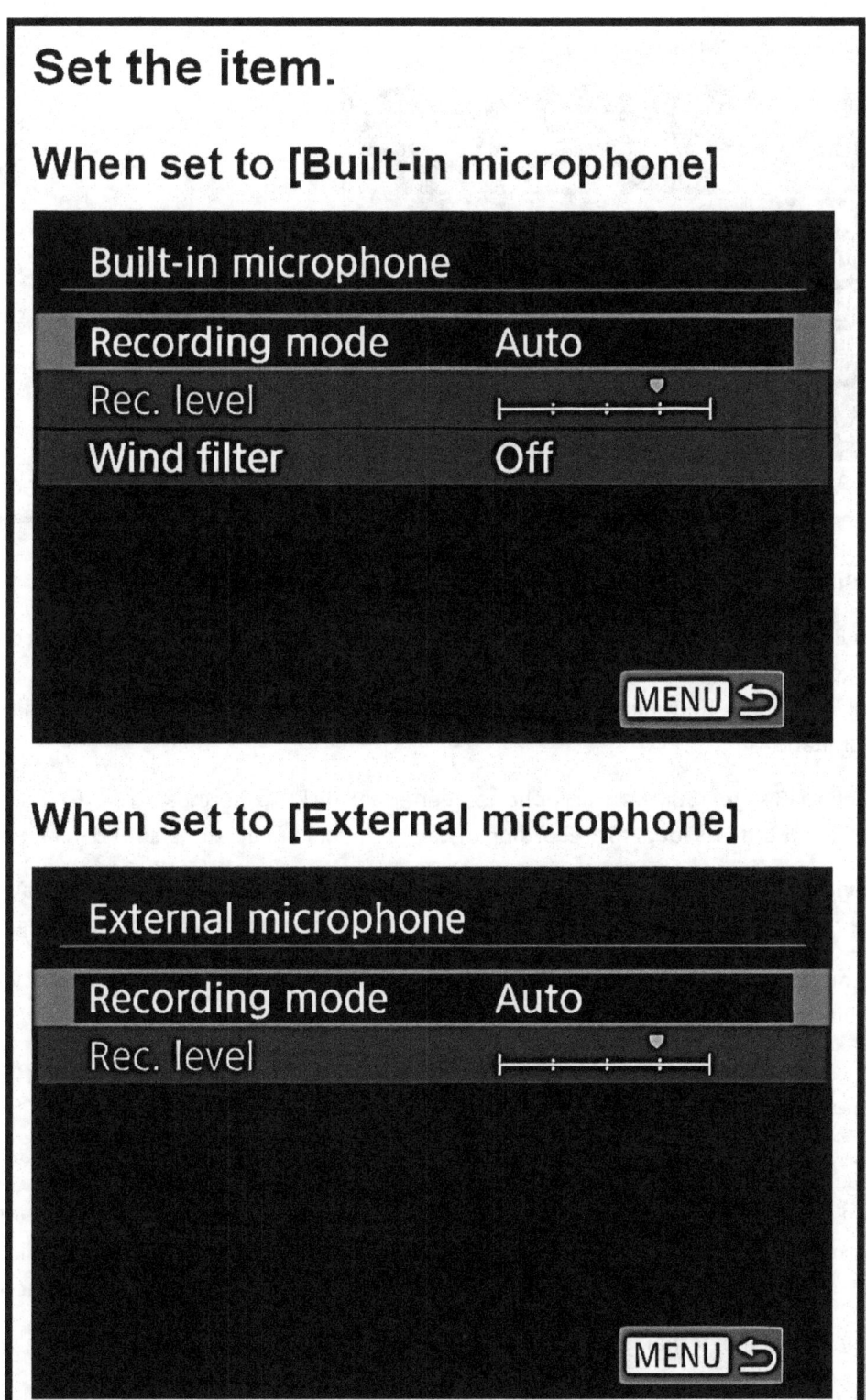

When set to [External microphone]

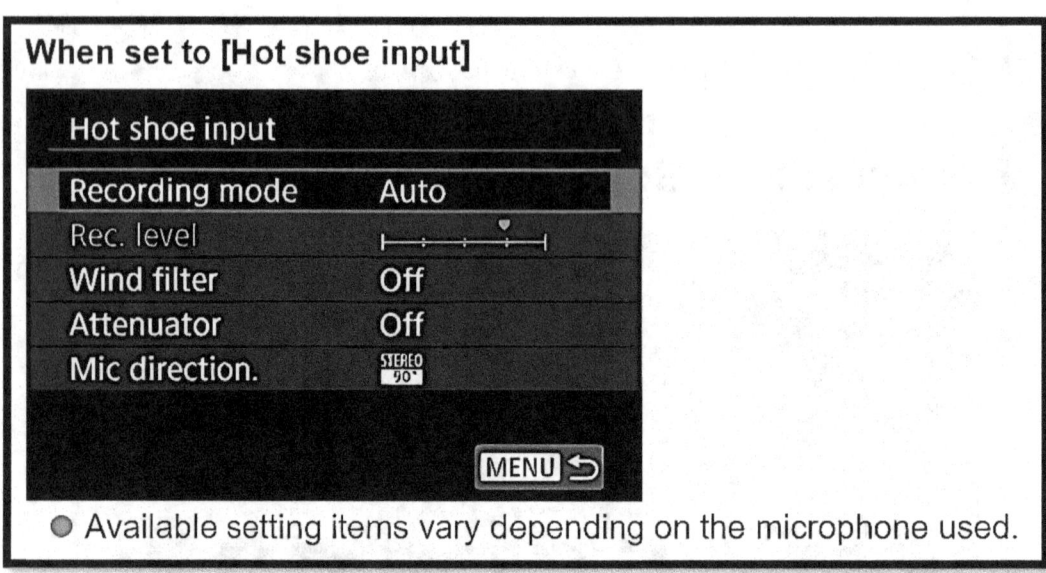

Using the Built-In Microphone

The Canon EOS R5 Mark II comes with a **built-in stereo microphone** that provides decent sound quality for general use. The built-in mic is convenient when an external microphone isn't available or practical, like when shooting spontaneous or casual videos. However, the built-in microphone has some limitations:

- **Limited Range**: Built-in microphones generally pick up sounds close to the camera, making them less ideal for recording distant subjects or capturing sound in large spaces.

- **Environmental Noise**: Since the built-in mic is close to the camera, it may capture handling noises, such as pressing buttons or adjusting settings during recording.

- **Wind Sensitivity**: As mentioned earlier, the built-in mic is sensitive to wind and environmental noises, which can reduce the clarity of outdoor recordings.

For these reasons, many videographers choose to use an **external microphone** to improve sound quality, especially in professional projects.

Using External Microphones for Better Audio Quality

The Canon EOS R5 Mark II has a 3.5mm microphone input jack, making it compatible with a wide range of external microphones. An external microphone can greatly enhance audio quality, reduce background noise, and capture clear sound even in noisy or spacious environments.

Here are the types of external microphones commonly used with the R5 Mark II, along with their recommended uses:

- **Lavalier (or Lapel) Microphone**: A lavalier microphone is a small, clip-on mic that can be attached to a speaker's clothing. Lav mics are ideal for interviews, vlogging, and situations where you want to record a single subject's voice clearly. Since it's close to the speaker's mouth, it minimizes background noise and captures clear audio even in crowded spaces.

- **Shotgun Microphone**: Shotgun microphones are highly directional mics that capture sound primarily from the front. This makes them great for recording specific sounds while reducing ambient noise from the sides or rear. Shotgun mics are often mounted on top of the camera or on a boom pole, making them useful for a range of situations like interviews, outdoor shoots, or film production.

- **Handheld Microphone**: A handheld microphone is useful in dynamic environments like live events, where the speaker might pass the mic between individuals. Handheld mics capture high-quality audio and are ideal for situations where the interviewer or speaker will be holding the mic directly.

- **Wireless Microphone Systems**: Wireless mics are especially useful for recording moving subjects. These systems often include a lavalier or handheld mic connected to a wireless transmitter, freeing up movement for the speaker while maintaining sound quality. Wireless mics are ideal for documentaries, interviews, and any setting where cables may be impractical.

Setting Up an External Microphone

To connect an external microphone to the EOS R5 Mark II, follow these steps:

- **Plug the Microphone into the 3.5mm Mic Jack**: Insert the microphone's 3.5mm plug into the microphone input on the side of the camera.

- **Adjust Audio Levels**: If you're using Manual audio control, check and adjust the audio levels according to the microphone's specifications.

- **Use the Sound Level Meter**: Once the microphone is connected, monitor audio levels on the screen. This will help you ensure that the sound is clear and within a safe range.

- **Test and Adjust**: Before beginning a full recording, perform a short test recording to check for clarity and adjust settings as needed.

Additional Tips for Using External Microphones

- **Use a Windscreen**: If you're recording outdoors, a windscreen or "deadcat" cover can minimize wind noise. These are often included with shotgun mics and are essential for clear outdoor recordings.

- **Monitor Audio with Headphones**: The R5 Mark II includes a headphone jack, allowing you to listen to audio in real-time. This is a great way to catch any issues with audio quality, such as unwanted background noise or clipping, before finalizing your recording.
- **Check Battery Levels**: Many external microphones require their own power source (such as AA batteries). Ensure your microphone has fresh batteries to avoid interruptions during recording.

Choosing the Right Microphone and Settings for Your Project

Selecting the right microphone and audio settings depends on the type of video you're creating:

- **Interviews and Vlogging**: For these projects, a lavalier microphone or a shotgun microphone works well. The lavalier provides consistent audio when the subject is stationary or moving slightly, while a shotgun mic is useful if the subject will be within a short distance of the camera.
- **Narrative Films**: Shotgun mics are often preferred for capturing directional audio without background noise, especially if the microphone is mounted on a boom pole. This setup allows precise control over the sound recorded from specific characters or scenes.
- **Documentary and Field Recording**: Wireless lavaliers or shotgun mics with windscreens are ideal in field settings. Wireless mics allow free movement, while shotgun mics help isolate specific sounds in noisy environments.
- **Live Events**: For live events, a handheld or wireless mic can capture interviews or presenter audio clearly. A shotgun mic can capture ambient sounds without the need to be directly on stage or next to the speaker.

Summing Up: Achieving Professional Audio with the Canon EOS R5 Mark II

Achieving great audio with the Canon EOS R5 Mark II requires understanding the camera's audio settings, choosing the right microphone, and making adjustments based on your environment. Here are some final takeaways:

- **Use Manual Control**: For consistent sound, especially in controlled environments, switch to manual audio control.
- **Monitor with Headphones**: Real-time monitoring allows you to catch audio issues before they impact the final recording.
- **Test and Adjust**: Run test recordings to fine-tune audio settings and microphone positioning, ensuring the best quality.

Conclusion

By mastering these audio features, you can enhance your videos with professional, high-quality sound, making your content more engaging and immersive for viewers.

CHAPTER 8

ADVANCED FEATURES FOR PROFESSIONALS

Dual Pixel RAW: Editing Flexibility

The Canon EOS R5 Mark II's **Dual Pixel RAW (DPR)** feature offers groundbreaking editing capabilities that enhance both the creative control and technical precision you have over your images. As both beginners and professionals explore this feature, it's essential to understand how DPR works, what makes it different from regular RAW files, and how to use it to make precise adjustments in post-processing. With Dual Pixel RAW, you can achieve fine-tuned control over aspects like sharpness, perspective, and light—giving you an edge in producing polished, high-quality images.

Understanding Dual Pixel RAW (DPR)

Dual Pixel RAW is a unique technology Canon introduced to capture and store additional depth and detail in RAW images. In traditional photography, each image sensor pixel captures a single point of light data. However, in Dual Pixel RAW, each pixel is split into two photodiodes, which work together to capture two slightly different angles of the same scene. This approach enables the camera to capture additional data, which can then be used for micro-adjustments in post-production.

In simpler terms, Dual Pixel RAW creates a "layered" version of your photograph, allowing you to make subtle adjustments to focus, lighting, and perspective after taking the shot. It's like adding an extra layer of editing flexibility that would otherwise require retaking the photo or advanced editing techniques.

Key Benefits of Dual Pixel RAW

Dual Pixel RAW offers three primary benefits in post-processing:

- **Microadjustments to Focus**: Dual Pixel RAW lets you fine-tune focus slightly after the photo has been taken. This can be helpful in portrait photography or macro shots where the focus point might need subtle correction to bring a subject's eye or another detail into sharper focus.

- **Bokeh Shift**: With Dual Pixel RAW, you can adjust the position of out-of-focus areas, like bokeh, in the background. This feature is particularly useful for controlling the composition of the background blur, allowing you to create more dynamic and visually pleasing images.

- **Ghosting Reduction**: Ghosting occurs when slight movements, such as leaves blowing in the wind, create double images or smudges in your photo. Dual Pixel RAW helps reduce this by allowing post-capture adjustments to minimize the effect of ghosting, creating cleaner, sharper images.

How to Activate Dual Pixel RAW on the Canon EOS R5 Mark II

To start using Dual Pixel RAW on your Canon EOS R5 Mark II, you'll first need to activate this setting within the camera's menu. Here's how:

- **Access the Menu**: Press the "Menu" button on your camera.

- **Select Image Quality Settings**: Navigate to the "Image Quality" settings within the camera's main shooting menu.

- **Enable Dual Pixel RAW**: Locate the "Dual Pixel RAW" option and set it to "On." When enabled, the camera will save images in Dual Pixel RAW format, which is slightly larger than standard RAW files due to the additional data.

Note: Since Dual Pixel RAW files are larger, they will take up more storage space and may require additional processing power. It's recommended to use a high-capacity memory card and to shoot in DPR only when you expect to need its specific adjustments.

Editing Dual Pixel RAW Files

Once you have captured images in Dual Pixel RAW format, the next step is to edit them. To fully unlock DPR's features, you'll need Canon's **Digital Photo Professional (DPP) software** or compatible editing software that supports DPR adjustments. Here's how each adjustment works within DPR:

1. **Focus Microadjustment**

   Focus microadjustment allows you to make small changes to the sharpness of specific areas within an image. This can be especially helpful when the focus is slightly off-center or if you want to emphasize a particular detail more prominently.

   How to Adjust Focus in Dual Pixel RAW:

   - Open your Dual Pixel RAW file in DPP.

   - Go to the "Dual Pixel RAW Optimizer" panel, which enables unique adjustments for DPR files.

   - Select the "Image Microadjustment" option.

- Use the slider to adjust the focus area; sliding left or right will shift focus within the image, allowing you to enhance the sharpness of specific details.

Tips for Effective Focus Adjustments:

- Keep adjustments minimal, as excessive shifting can result in a loss of image quality.
- Focus adjustments are ideal for portraits, where you may want to enhance sharpness in the subject's eyes or other prominent features.

2. **Bokeh Shift**

Bokeh shift is another powerful tool in Dual Pixel RAW that lets you subtly reposition the blurred areas in an image, usually the background, to refine composition or to improve the balance between the subject and background.

How to Apply Bokeh Shift in Dual Pixel RAW:

- In the "Dual Pixel RAW Optimizer," select the "Bokeh Shift" option.
- Use the on-screen controls to shift the bokeh effect horizontally or vertically, adjusting the blurred areas around the main subject.

Tips for Effective Bokeh Adjustments:

- Use this adjustment to guide the viewer's attention towards the main subject.
- Bokeh shift is especially useful in portrait photography, where you may want to enhance or slightly change the background composition without affecting the subject itself.

3. **Ghosting Reduction**

Ghosting reduction allows you to minimize the appearance of unwanted "ghosting" artifacts in images. These are often caused by slight movements, like moving leaves or a subject shifting slightly during the shot.

How to Reduce Ghosting in Dual Pixel RAW:

- Open the DPR file in DPP and go to the "Dual Pixel RAW Optimizer."
- Select the "Ghosting Reduction" option.
- Use the slider to adjust the ghosting effect; this will subtly minimize unwanted artifacts and help produce a clearer image.

Tips for Effective Ghosting Reduction:

- Use ghosting reduction sparingly, as it may introduce slight blur in surrounding areas.
- Ghosting reduction works best in outdoor scenes with moving elements, such as leaves, water, or other organic textures.

Practical Applications of Dual Pixel RAW for Professionals

For professionals, Dual Pixel RAW offers unique advantages in various photography genres:

- **Portrait Photography**: DPR's microadjustment and bokeh shift options are invaluable in portrait work. These tools help achieve the perfect focus on the subject's eyes, refine the background bokeh, and ensure that each shot is visually appealing.

- **Macro Photography**: In macro photography, slight shifts in focus can make a significant difference. With DPR, photographers can fine-tune focus and reduce ghosting artifacts, ensuring a clean and crisp final image.

- **Landscape Photography**: When shooting landscapes, ghosting reduction is useful for minimizing movement artifacts, such as leaves or grass swaying in the wind, enhancing overall sharpness and clarity.

Optimizing Your Workflow with Dual Pixel RAW

Because DPR files are larger and more demanding on processing resources, it's important to optimize your workflow for efficient editing. Here are some tips for handling Dual Pixel RAW files:

- **Use a Fast Memory Card**: A high-speed SD or CFexpress card is essential for handling larger DPR files without delays.

- **Save DPR Edits in Stages**: Since DPR files can be memory-intensive, it's helpful to save adjustments in stages rather than attempting all at once. This can prevent software lag and ensure that you achieve the best results.

- **Backup Originals**: Since DPR editing modifies the RAW data itself, it's a good idea to keep a backup of the original files. This way, you can revert to the original if you want to make different adjustments.

Common Questions About Dual Pixel RAW

- **Does Dual Pixel RAW Reduce Image Quality?**

No, DPR doesn't reduce quality; instead, it adds editing flexibility. However, large adjustments can reduce the subtlety of the effects, so it's best to make minimal, precise adjustments.

- **Is Dual Pixel RAW Needed for Every Photo?**

Not necessarily. Use DPR when you anticipate needing adjustments to focus, background bokeh, or ghosting. For general photography, regular RAW will be sufficient and easier to manage.

- **Does Dual Pixel RAW Affect Shooting Speed?**

Yes, due to the larger file size, shooting in DPR may result in slower write speeds and a reduced buffer capacity. Use DPR selectively in situations where you'll benefit from the added control.

Conclusion

Dual Pixel RAW on the Canon EOS R5 Mark II empowers photographers to make fine adjustments to their images in post-production, offering a level of flexibility that can be particularly useful in professional projects. By enabling focus microadjustment, bokeh shift, and ghosting reduction, Dual Pixel RAW provides unique tools that elevate image quality and creative control.

As you become familiar with using Dual Pixel RAW, you'll find that this feature enables you to achieve more polished, professional results, especially in challenging shooting conditions. Whether you're refining portraits, perfecting macro shots, or capturing dynamic landscapes, Dual Pixel RAW can help you take your photography to the next level.

What is In-Body Image Stabilization (IBIS)?

In simple terms, **In-Body Image Stabilization (IBIS)** is a technology that stabilizes the camera's sensor to reduce or eliminate the blur caused by small hand movements. When taking photos or recording video, even minor movements can result in noticeable image blur or shaky footage. IBIS works by compensating for these tiny movements, enabling you to capture sharper images and smoother videos even without a tripod.

Unlike lens-based stabilization, which works by stabilizing the lens elements, IBIS stabilizes the camera sensor itself. This sensor-shift technology is embedded within the camera body, giving you stabilization with virtually any lens you attach to the camera, whether or not the lens has its own stabilization feature.

How Does IBIS Work?

The Canon EOS R5 Mark II's IBIS system works using gyroscopic sensors that detect even the slightest hand movements or shifts. When these sensors pick up on movement, they send signals to the camera's microprocessor, which then directs tiny motors to move the sensor in the opposite direction. This counteraction keeps the sensor stable, minimizing motion blur and shake.

IBIS in the EOS R5 Mark II offers **up to 8 stops of stabilization**, meaning it can handle significant movement before blur appears in your shots. This stabilization power is particularly beneficial for low-light photography, handheld shooting, and any situation where using a tripod might not be feasible or practical.

Benefits of IBIS in the Canon EOS R5 Mark II

Understanding the benefits of IBIS can help you take advantage of its full potential in various shooting scenarios. Here are some primary advantages of using IBIS on the EOS R5 Mark II:

- **Sharper Images in Low Light Conditions**: When shooting in low light, your camera typically needs a slower shutter speed to capture enough light, which increases the risk of hand-shake blur. With IBIS, you can achieve sharp images even at slower shutter speeds, allowing you to capture nightscapes, dimly lit interiors, or sunset shots with ease.

- **Stability for Handheld Shooting**: Not all situations allow for the use of a tripod, such as when shooting on the move, in crowded areas, or in tight spaces. IBIS provides stability for handheld shooting, allowing you to capture still shots and smooth videos without additional support.

- **Compatible with Non-Stabilized Lenses**: Some prime lenses and other specialty lenses lack built-in stabilization. With IBIS, you can use these lenses confidently, knowing that the camera's stabilization will support you.

- **Improved Video Footage**: For videographers, IBIS significantly enhances handheld video recording by reducing shake and jitter. It's especially useful for creating smooth, cinematic motion without the need for bulky stabilization rigs.

- **Enhanced Creativity and Flexibility**: With IBIS, you have more creative freedom to experiment with different shutter speeds and apertures. You can try long exposure techniques, shoot in challenging conditions, and capture fast-moving subjects without compromising stability.

Maximizing IBIS Performance on the EOS R5 Mark II

To get the most out of the Canon EOS R5 Mark II's IBIS, you'll want to understand how to set it up and how to adapt it to different shooting scenarios.

Setting Up IBIS on the Canon EOS R5 Mark II

The EOS R5 Mark II's IBIS can be enabled or disabled within the camera's menu. Here's how to set it up:

- **Access the Menu**: Press the "Menu" button on the back of the camera.
- **Navigate to Image Stabilization Settings**: Under the "Shoot" tab, look for "IS Settings" or "Image Stabilizer."
- **Enable or Disable IBIS**: Here, you can choose to enable or disable IBIS, depending on your needs. Generally, enabling IBIS is ideal for most handheld shooting scenarios.

When to Use IBIS

Knowing when to use IBIS and when to turn it off is essential for capturing the best results.

- **Low-Light Situations**: When shooting in low light, enable IBIS to counteract camera shake caused by slower shutter speeds.
- **Handheld Photography and Video**: For handheld shooting, IBIS helps keep your shots steady, whether you're shooting stills or recording video.
- **Long Exposure**: With IBIS, you can experiment with longer exposure times, creating artistic images with blurred motion in the background while keeping the main subject sharp.
- **Telephoto Lenses**: Using long lenses amplifies even the smallest shakes. With IBIS, you can shoot sharper images even with telephoto lenses, making it an invaluable tool for wildlife, sports, and portrait photography.

When to Turn Off IBIS

Although IBIS is beneficial in most situations, there are cases when turning it off can produce better results:

- **When Using a Tripod**: When your camera is mounted on a tripod, the stability is already taken care of, and IBIS may introduce slight jitter as it tries to compensate for non-existent movement.
- **Panning Shots**: In panning photography, such as tracking a moving subject, the IBIS may interfere with the horizontal movement. For these shots, turning IBIS off ensures smoother, more natural motion blur.
- **High Shutter Speeds**: If you're shooting at high shutter speeds (e.g., 1/1000s or faster), IBIS may not be necessary, as these speeds inherently reduce the risk of shake.

Using IBIS with Different Lenses

One of the biggest advantages of IBIS in the EOS R5 Mark II is that it works with virtually any lens, giving you stabilization even with lenses that lack Optical Image Stabilization (OIS). However, when paired with lenses that have their own OIS, the EOS R5 Mark II uses a **coordinated IS system**, combining both in-lens and in-body stabilization for optimal results.

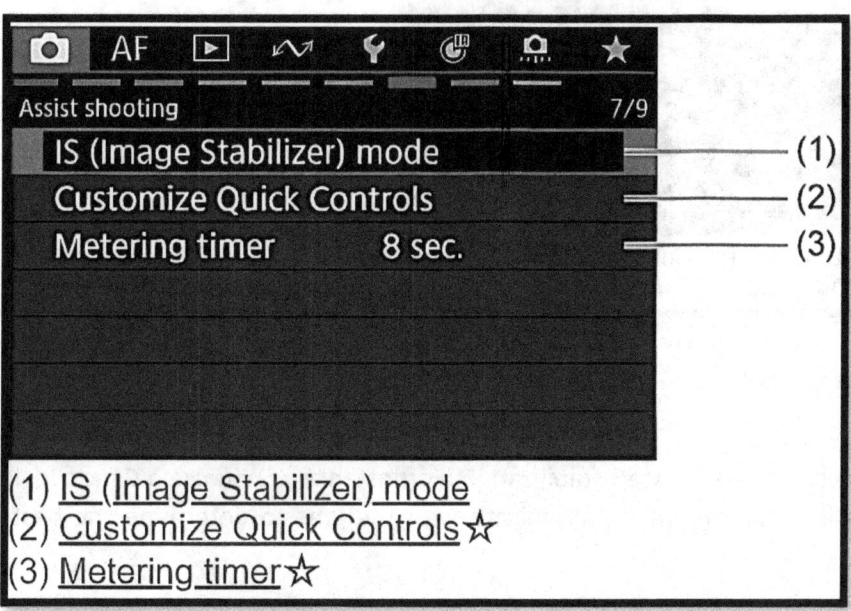

(1) IS (Image Stabilizer) mode
(2) Customize Quick Controls ☆
(3) Metering timer ☆

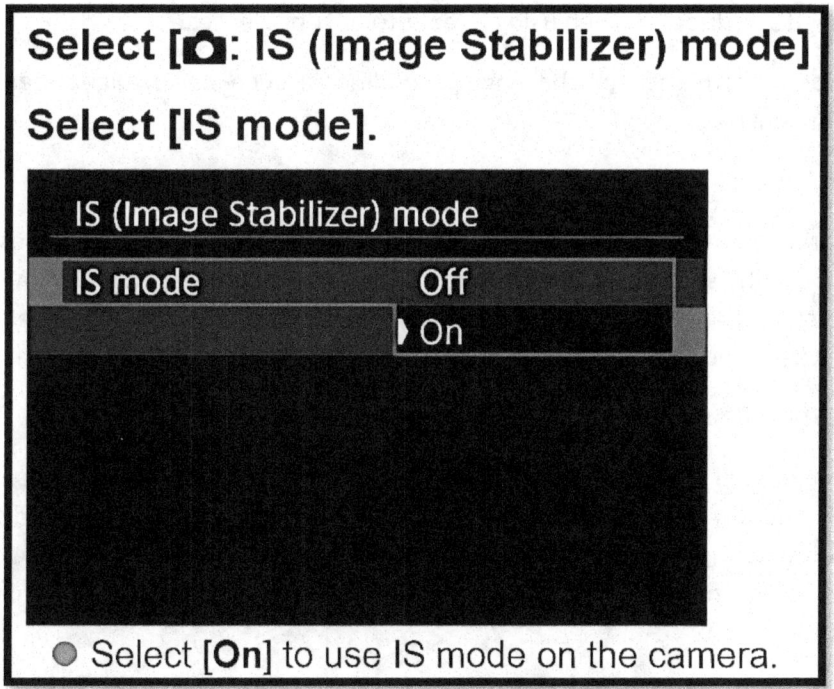

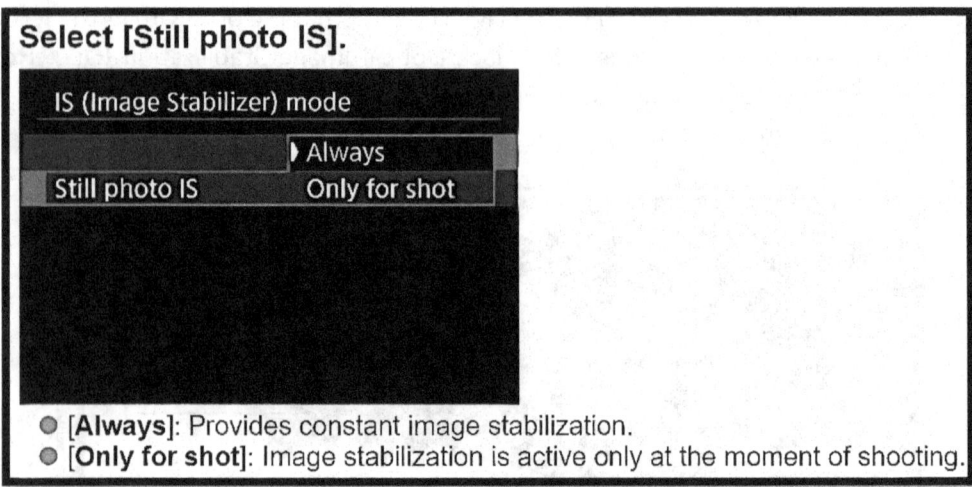

How Coordinated IS Works

Coordinated IS is a system where the camera's IBIS works in tandem with the lens's stabilization mechanism to provide enhanced stabilization. For instance, if you use a Canon RF lens with OIS, the camera's IBIS system will communicate with the lens to determine the best stabilization approach.

Benefits of Coordinated IS:

- Increased stabilization when using telephoto or zoom lenses.
- Superior performance in challenging conditions, such as low-light scenes or windy environments.

IBIS and Prime Lenses

When using prime lenses or lenses without built-in stabilization, IBIS becomes even more valuable. For example, shooting handheld with a 50mm prime lens at a slower shutter speed is easier and sharper, thanks to IBIS. This flexibility opens up possibilities for creative handheld photography, where you can maintain clarity without sacrificing flexibility in lens choice.

Using IBIS for Video Recording

For videographers, IBIS offers substantial benefits, especially when recording handheld video. Video requires smooth, steady footage, and the EOS R5 Mark II's IBIS is designed to keep your shots stable without the need for additional equipment. This stability is critical for creating a professional look and feel to your videos, allowing for steady footage even while walking or tracking a subject.

Additional Video Stabilization with Digital IS

In addition to the hardware-based IBIS, the EOS R5 Mark II also includes a **Digital IS** feature, which uses software to add an extra layer of stability to video footage. Digital IS can be combined with IBIS for enhanced results, especially if you're recording while moving. However, keep in mind that using Digital IS crops the frame slightly, so consider this if framing is crucial.

Steps for Enabling Digital IS in Video:

- **Enter Video Mode**: Switch your camera to video mode.

- **Access the IS Settings**: Go to the menu and find the "Digital IS" option under video settings.

- **Enable Digital IS**: Choose either "Standard" or "Enhanced." "Enhanced" provides stronger stabilization but with a greater crop.

Tips for Optimizing IBIS Performance

- **Hold the Camera Steady**: Although IBIS compensates for hand movements, a steady hand always improves stability. Use proper grip techniques, keeping your elbows close to your body for added support.

- **Experiment with Shutter Speeds**: Try slower shutter speeds than you would usually use for handheld shots to take full advantage of IBIS. For instance, if you usually avoid anything slower than 1/60s, IBIS may allow you to shoot at 1/15s or even slower with clear results.

- **Pair with Compatible Lenses for Best Results**: For best performance, use RF lenses with in-lens stabilization. Coordinated IS provides the most effective stabilization and ensures the camera and lens work seamlessly together.

Limitations of IBIS

While IBIS is highly beneficial, it does have some limitations:

- **Limited Impact on Fast Motion**: IBIS is excellent for reducing hand-shake blur but less effective for fast-moving subjects. For action photography, a fast shutter speed is still necessary.

- **Slight Noise**: Some photographers may notice a slight noise from the IBIS mechanism when it's active, though this is typically subtle and unlikely to affect most shooting situations.

Conclusion

In-body Image Stabilization on the Canon EOS R5 Mark II provides remarkable stability and clarity for handheld shooting, giving both beginners and professionals the freedom to explore creative techniques and challenging environments. By understanding how to set up IBIS, when to use it, and how to optimize it for different lenses and shooting conditions, you can maximize its potential, transforming handheld photography and videography into a much more rewarding experience.

Focus Stacking and Advanced Image Processing

Focus stacking and advanced image processing are powerful features for photographers, especially those working with macro, landscape, and product photography. The Canon EOS R5 Mark II offers these capabilities to help capture every detail in a scene, from the closest foreground to the farthest background. In this section, we'll explore what focus stacking is, how it works, and how advanced image processing can elevate your photography, giving both beginners and professionals the skills needed to master these features on the EOS R5 Mark II.

What is Focus Stacking?

Focus stacking is a technique that combines multiple images taken at different focus points to create one final image with a greater depth of field than would be possible in a single shot. Depth of field refers to the portion of an image that appears sharp from foreground to background, and in some scenes, a single focus point can't capture everything clearly. Focus stacking solves this problem by allowing photographers to take a series of images, each focused on different parts of the subject, and then merge them to create an image where everything is in focus.

Why Use Focus Stacking?

Focus stacking is valuable for several reasons:

- **Macro Photography**: In close-up photography, the depth of field can be very shallow, even when using a narrow aperture. Focus stacking allows you to capture small details up close, making sure every part of the subject is sharp.

- **Landscape Photography**: When photographing a landscape scene, you may want both the foreground (such as rocks or flowers) and the distant background (like mountains) to be in focus. Focus stacking can achieve this by ensuring every part of the scene is sharp and detailed.

- **Product Photography**: For professional product shots, focus stacking makes sure every part of the product is sharp and clear, highlighting textures, details, and quality.

How Focus Stacking Works on the Canon EOS R5 Mark II

Focus stacking on the Canon EOS R5 Mark II involves two main steps:

- **Capture Multiple Images at Different Focus Points**: In the field, you take multiple shots of the same scene with slight adjustments in focus, from the nearest point to the farthest.

- **Merge Images in Post-Processing Software**: After capturing your images, you use photo-editing software to merge them, creating a single image with a broad depth of field.

Step-by-Step Guide to Using Focus Stacking on the Canon EOS R5 Mark II

Step 1: Setting Up Your Camera

Before capturing your focus-stacked images, make sure your camera is set up for the highest quality results.

- **Switch to Manual Focus Mode**: Manual focus allows you to control exactly where each focus point lands for each shot.

- **Use a Tripod**: Keeping your camera steady is essential. Using a tripod helps ensure that each shot remains consistent in composition, avoiding alignment issues in post-processing.

- **Set Aperture and Exposure**: Set your camera to a narrower aperture (higher f-stop, like f/8 or f/11) for better depth of field, but remember that focus stacking will compensate for shallow depth of field in close-up work. Use consistent exposure settings for each shot.

- **Enable Live View**: For precise focus adjustments, switch to Live View mode, which allows you to zoom in on specific areas of the scene as you adjust the focus.

Step 2: Capturing the Images

With the camera set up, you're ready to begin capturing the sequence of images that will be used for the focus stack:

- **Start with the Closest Point**: Begin by focusing on the nearest part of the subject or scene that you want in focus.

- **Adjust Focus Gradually**: After capturing the first image, slightly adjust the focus to move farther into the scene and take the next shot. Repeat this process, moving the focus further with each shot until you reach the farthest point you want in focus.

- **Take Multiple Shots**: Depending on the depth of the scene, you may need anywhere from a few images to dozens to achieve full focus from front to back. For complex scenes, more images ensure complete coverage.

Step 3: Merging the Images in Post-Processing

Once you have your series of images, the next step is to combine them in editing software. Adobe Photoshop and specialized software like Helicon Focus are popular choices for focus stacking.

- **Import Images into Software**: Open all the focus-stacked images in your chosen editing software.
- **Align the Images**: Even if you used a tripod, there may be slight shifts between images. Use the alignment tool to ensure the images are perfectly matched.
- **Apply Focus Stacking**: Use the focus-stacking tool to blend the images. This feature automatically selects the sharpest areas from each image and merges them into a single, focused image.
- **Make Final Adjustments**: After stacking, you may need to make small tweaks for color, contrast, and other finishing touches.

Advanced Image Processing on the Canon EOS R5 Mark II

In addition to focus stacking, the Canon EOS R5 Mark II offers several advanced image processing features that can enhance your photography. These include HDR (High Dynamic Range) shooting, in-camera RAW processing, and Dual Pixel RAW adjustments.

HDR Mode: Capturing High Dynamic Range

HDR (High Dynamic Range) captures a broader range of brightness levels than a standard image, allowing details to be preserved in both the darkest and brightest parts of the scene. This is particularly useful in high-contrast situations, like sunset photography, where both the sky and the foreground have details you want to retain.

How to Use HDR Mode

- **Enable HDR Mode**: In your camera's menu, find the HDR setting and turn it on.
- **Select HDR Settings**: The EOS R5 Mark II allows you to choose between automatic HDR or a specific level of HDR strength (e.g., low, medium, high). Higher HDR settings increase the range of brightness but may look more artificial.
- **Capture the Image**: When you press the shutter, the camera will take three consecutive shots at different exposures and blend them automatically.

In-Camera RAW Processing

For photographers who shoot in RAW format, the EOS R5 Mark II's **in-camera RAW processing** feature allows you to make edits directly on the camera without needing a computer. This can save time and provides a way to make basic adjustments on the go.

Using In-Camera RAW Processing

- **Select the RAW Image**: In the playback menu, choose a RAW image you'd like to edit.
- **Choose Processing Options**: You can adjust settings like exposure, white balance, picture style, and sharpness.
- **Save the Edited Image**: Once you're happy with the adjustments, save a copy of the edited image in JPEG format.

Dual Pixel RAW: Enhanced Editing Control

Dual Pixel RAW is a unique feature that captures additional depth information in each image, allowing for small adjustments in focus, bokeh, and shadow areas in post-processing.

Benefits of Dual Pixel RAW

- **Micro-Adjustment of Focus**: Dual Pixel RAW allows you to shift the focus slightly after the shot has been taken, helping you make micro-adjustments to the sharpness in specific areas.
- **Bokeh Shift**: You can slightly adjust the background blur to make it more or less pronounced.
- **Ghosting Reduction**: In certain lighting conditions, Dual Pixel RAW can help reduce ghosting and glare effects, enhancing image clarity.

Processing Dual Pixel RAW Images

Dual Pixel RAW images need specialized software, such as Canon's Digital Photo Professional (DPP), to access the advanced adjustments.

Tips for Maximizing Focus Stacking and Advanced Image Processing

- **Plan Your Shot Carefully**: Especially for focus stacking, consider the depth and complexity of your subject. Fewer images are needed for simple compositions, while more images will be needed for complex, layered scenes.
- **Practice with HDR and Dual Pixel RAW**: Experimenting with HDR and Dual Pixel RAW features can help you determine when and how these options enhance your shots.
- **Use Quality Post-Processing Software**: While Canon's in-camera tools are powerful, you'll get the best results from advanced software like Adobe Lightroom or Photoshop for focus stacking and RAW processing.

When to Use Focus Stacking and Advanced Image Processing

Understanding when to use focus stacking, HDR, in-camera RAW processing, and Dual Pixel RAW will elevate your photography and ensure you capture the best possible images in various scenarios:

- **Macro Photography**: Use focus stacking to ensure that all intricate details are sharp.
- **Landscape Photography**: For wide scenes with both near and far elements, use focus stacking and HDR to capture detail and dynamic range.
- **Portraits and Product Photography**: Dual Pixel RAW allows for subtle adjustments to focus and bokeh, helping to fine-tune portraits and product shots.
- **Low Light or High Contrast Scenes**: HDR is ideal for situations where you want to capture detail in both shadows and highlights, such as sunrise or sunset photography.

Conclusion

Focus stacking and advanced image processing tools on the Canon EOS R5 Mark II open up new possibilities for creating sharp, detailed, and high-quality images across various photography styles. For both beginners and professionals, understanding these features allows for greater creative flexibility, ensuring that every shot is as polished and dynamic as possible. Through consistent practice and experimentation, these advanced capabilities can become integral parts of your photography skill set, taking your work to the next level with the EOS R5 Mark II.

CHAPTER 9

WIRELESS CONNECTIVITY AND SHARING

Wi-Fi and Bluetooth Pairing for Remote Control

The Canon EOS R5 Mark II is equipped with advanced wireless connectivity options that allow you to pair your camera with a smartphone, tablet, or computer. This pairing opens up powerful remote control capabilities, giving photographers and videographers greater flexibility, convenience, and creative opportunities. In this section, we'll explore the key concepts of Wi-Fi and Bluetooth pairing, why they're important, and provide a step-by-step guide to setting them up.

Why Use Wi-Fi and Bluetooth for Remote Control?

Wi-Fi and Bluetooth connectivity transform the way you interact with your camera by enabling wireless control. Here's why these features are invaluable:

- **Convenience**:

    Adjust settings, capture images, or record video remotely without physically interacting with the camera.

- **Enhanced Creativity**:

    Position your camera in hard-to-reach places, such as high angles or tight spaces, and control it effortlessly.

- **Live View Monitoring**:

    Use your smartphone or tablet as a live monitor, ideal for precise framing and focusing.

- **Seamless Sharing**:

    Instantly transfer images and videos to your device for quick sharing on social media or cloud platforms.

Understanding Wi-Fi and Bluetooth Connectivity

Bluetooth:

Bluetooth provides a low-energy connection that maintains continuous communication between the camera and paired device. It is primarily used for:

- Quick pairing.
- Triggering the camera remotely.

- Geotagging images using your device's GPS.

Wi-Fi:

Wi-Fi is used for more data-intensive tasks, including:

- Viewing and transferring high-resolution images or videos.
- Full remote control of the camera via the Canon Camera Connect app.
- Firmware updates and cloud backups.

Wi-Fi and Bluetooth often work together for an optimized experience. Bluetooth establishes the initial link, while Wi-Fi handles larger data transfers or advanced functions.

Getting Started: Preparing Your Camera

Before pairing, ensure your Canon EOS R5 Mark II and device are ready:

- **Charge Your Devices**:

  Ensure both your camera and the device you're pairing with (smartphone, tablet, etc.) have sufficient battery power.

- **Install the Canon Camera Connect App**:

  Download and install the Canon Camera Connect app, available on both iOS and Android platforms.

- **Enable Wireless Functions**:

  On your camera, go to the *Menu* and navigate to the *Wireless Communication Settings*.

Step-by-Step Guide to Bluetooth Pairing

Bluetooth pairing is quick and ideal for basic remote operations like triggering the shutter or maintaining a constant connection.

- **Turn On Bluetooth**:
    - On your camera, access the *Menu > Wireless Communication Settings > Bluetooth Settings*.
    - Set Bluetooth to *Enable*.

- **Pair Your Device**:
    - Open the Canon Camera Connect app on your smartphone or tablet.
    - In the app, select *Add Camera* and follow the on-screen instructions.

- **Authorize the Pairing**:
    - The camera will display a pairing request. Confirm the connection by selecting *OK*.
    - On your device, accept the pairing request to establish the link.
- **Verify Connection**:
    Once paired, your device will appear in the camera's Bluetooth menu. You can now use the app to trigger the shutter or geotag images.

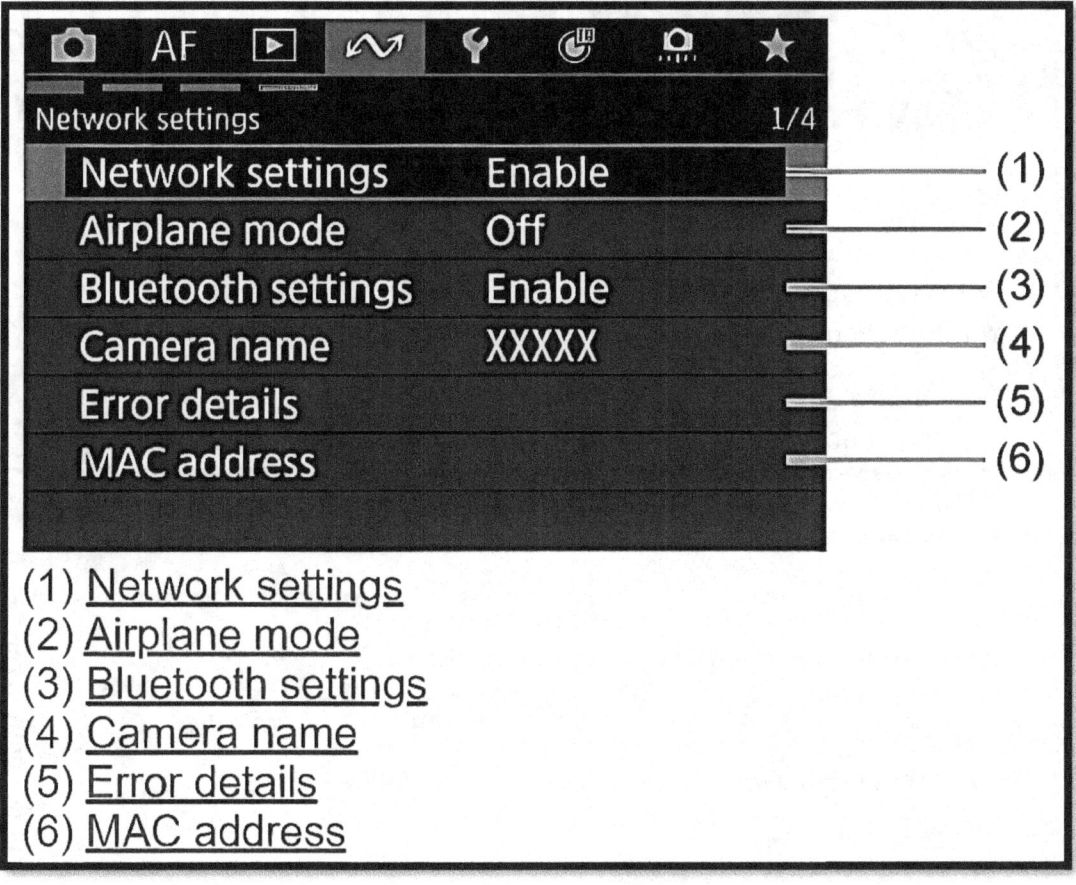

(1) Network settings
(2) Airplane mode
(3) Bluetooth settings
(4) Camera name
(5) Error details
(6) MAC address

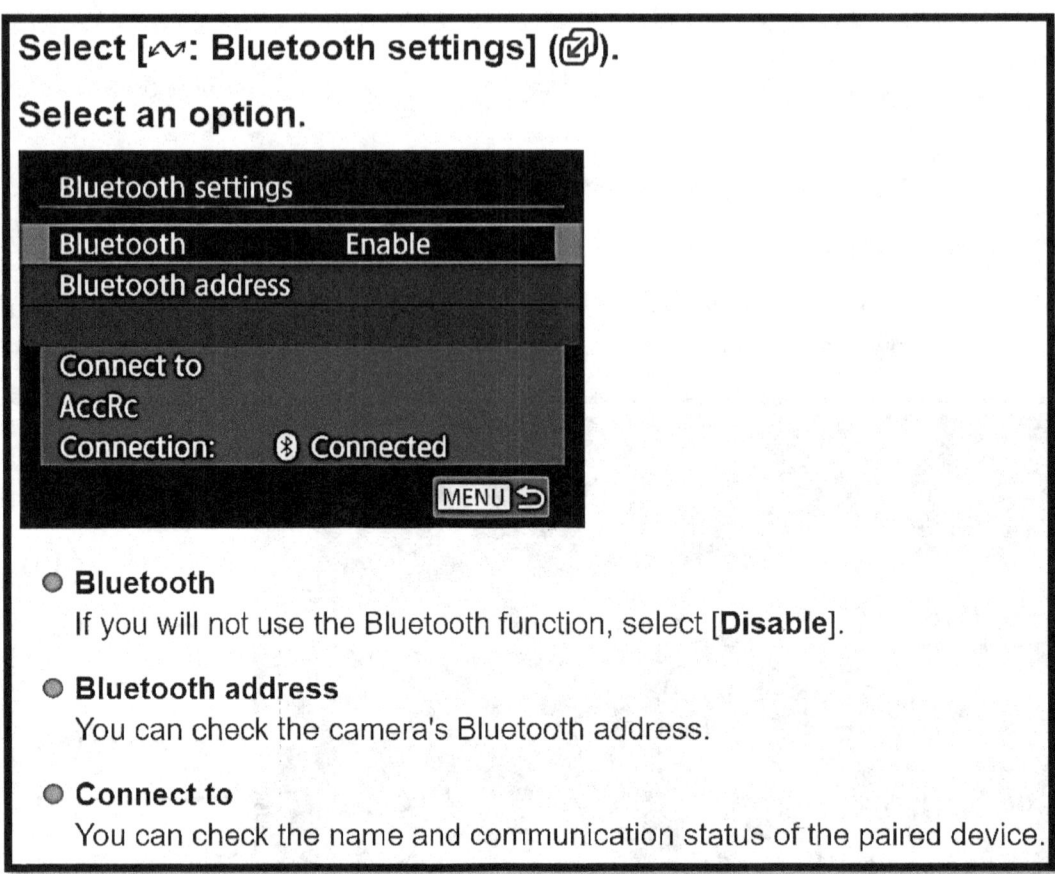

Step-by-Step Guide to Wi-Fi Pairing

Wi-Fi pairing enables more advanced functions, such as full remote control and image transfers.

- **Activate Wi-Fi on the Camera**:
    - Go to *Menu > Wireless Communication Settings > Wi-Fi Settings*.
    - Set Wi-Fi to *Enable*.
- **Select Connection Type**:
    - Choose *Wi-Fi Function > Connect to Smartphone*.
    - Select *Easy Connection*.
- **Connect via App**:
    - Open the Canon Camera Connect app on your smartphone or tablet.

- o   Follow the app's instructions to connect to the camera's Wi-Fi network.
- **Confirm the Connection**:

    The app will display the camera's name. Select it to finalize the connection.

- **Test the Setup**:

    In the app, try accessing the *Remote Live View Shooting* feature. You should see the camera's live view feed on your device.

Using the Remote Control Features

Remote Shutter Release:

Use the app to trigger the camera's shutter from a distance, ideal for group photos, long exposures, or wildlife photography.

Live View Monitoring:

The app displays the camera's live view feed, allowing you to adjust focus, exposure, and framing directly from your device.

Adjust Camera Settings:

Change key settings like aperture, shutter speed, ISO, and white balance via the app, providing full control remotely.

Start/Stop Video Recording:

Begin or stop video recording through the app, especially useful when shooting interviews or vlogs where you're in front of the camera.

Troubleshooting Pairing Issues

Wireless connectivity issues can occur, but most problems have simple solutions:

- **Connection Fails to Establish**:
    - o   Ensure both the camera and device have Bluetooth and Wi-Fi enabled.
    - o   Check that the Canon Camera Connect app is updated to the latest version.
- **Frequent Disconnections**:
    - o   Keep the camera and device within range (approximately 10 meters for Bluetooth and 30 meters for Wi-Fi).
    - o   Avoid environments with excessive wireless interference.

- **Device Not Recognized**:
    - Forget the camera in your device's Bluetooth or Wi-Fi settings and reattempt pairing.
    - Restart both the camera and the paired device.
- **App Crashes or Freezes**:

    Update the app and ensure your device's operating system is compatible.

Maximizing Connectivity Performance

- **Keep Firmware Updated**:

    Regular firmware updates enhance connectivity features and fix known bugs.

- **Optimize Device Settings**:

    On your smartphone, disable background apps that may interfere with the Canon Camera Connect app.

- **Use a Dedicated Device**:

    For professional workflows, consider using a dedicated tablet or smartphone for camera pairing to reduce interruptions.

Practical Scenarios for Remote Control

- **Self-Portraits and Group Photos:**

    Place the camera on a tripod, frame the shot via the app, and trigger the shutter remotely.

- **Wildlife Photography:**

    Position the camera near the subject and control it from a safe distance, avoiding disturbances.

- **Astrophotography:**

    Use the app to adjust settings and capture long exposures without touching the camera, reducing vibrations.

- **Event Coverage:**

    Monitor and control multiple cameras remotely for seamless event documentation.

Conclusion

Wi-Fi and Bluetooth pairing on the Canon EOS R5 Mark II open up a world of possibilities for photographers and videographers. From simple remote shutter operations to advanced live view monitoring and setting adjustments, these wireless features make capturing the perfect shot easier and more efficient. By understanding the setup process and troubleshooting common issues, you can unlock the full potential of your camera's connectivity features and take your photography to new heights.

Transferring Images via Canon Camera Connect App

The Canon Camera Connect app is an essential tool for users of the Canon EOS R5 Mark II who want a seamless way to transfer images from their camera to their smartphone or tablet. This feature is beneficial for photographers and videographers looking to quickly share their work or edit on the go. In this section, we'll explore why transferring images through the app is advantageous, the steps to set it up, and practical use cases for both beginners and professionals.

Why Use the Canon Camera Connect App for Image Transfer?

Transferring images via the Canon Camera Connect app offers several key advantages over traditional methods like cables or card readers:

- **Convenience**:

  Wireless transfer eliminates the need for cables or additional equipment, making it faster and easier.

- **Immediate Sharing**:

  Share your images directly to social media, email, or cloud platforms without needing a computer.

- **Selective Transfers**:

  The app lets you browse and choose specific images or videos to transfer, saving time and storage space.

- **Supports Multiple Formats**:

  Transfer images in JPEG, HEIF, or even RAW formats, depending on your needs.

- **On-the-Go Editing**:

  Move images to your smartphone for quick edits using photo editing apps, especially useful for professionals delivering images in real-time.

Preparing Your Camera and Device

Before you begin transferring images, there are a few steps to prepare your Canon EOS R5 Mark II and your smartphone or tablet:

- **Install the Canon Camera Connect App**:

    Download the app from the Apple App Store or Google Play Store and install it on your device.

- **Check Battery Levels**:

    Ensure your camera and smartphone have sufficient battery charge to avoid interruptions.

- **Enable Wireless Communication on the Camera**:

    Navigate to *Menu > Wireless Communication Settings* and enable both Wi-Fi and Bluetooth.

- **Organize Your Media**:

    Review the images on your camera and delete any you don't need to avoid clutter during the transfer process.

Setting Up the Connection

Step 1: Turn On Wi-Fi on Your Camera

- On your Canon EOS R5 Mark II, go to *Menu > Wi-Fi/Bluetooth Settings*.
- Enable Wi-Fi and select *Wi-Fi Function > Connect to Smartphone*.

Step 2: Select Connection Method

- Choose *Easy Connection* to generate a unique Wi-Fi network that your smartphone can join.
- The camera will display the network name (SSID) and password.

Step 3: Connect Your Smartphone to the Camera's Wi-Fi

- Open your smartphone's Wi-Fi settings.
- Locate the camera's network name and connect using the password provided.

Step 4: Open the Canon Camera Connect App

- Once connected, launch the app.
- The app will automatically detect your camera and establish a link.

Step 5: Authorize the Connection

- On the camera's screen, confirm the connection request by selecting *OK*.

Transferring Images

Once your camera and smartphone are paired, you can transfer images through the app using the following steps:

Option 1: View and Select Images

- Open the Canon Camera Connect app and tap *Images on Camera*.
- Browse through the thumbnails of your stored images and videos.
- Select one or multiple files for transfer by tapping on them.

Option 2: Auto-Transfer Feature

Enable the auto-transfer option in the app settings to automatically send newly captured images to your device in real time. This is useful for live events or instant social media updates.

Option 3: Transfer RAW Files

If you're transferring RAW images for professional editing, ensure your smartphone hasan app that supports RAW file handling.

Option 4: Bulk Transfers

For a large number of images, select *All Images* in the app to transfer them in bulk. Note that this may take longer depending on file sizes.

Customizing Transfer Settings

The Canon Camera Connect app provides several options to tailor your transfer experience:

- **Image Format**:

Choose between JPEG, HEIF, or RAW, depending on your file requirements.

- **Image Size**:

Opt to resize large images before transfer to save storage space on your smartphone.

- **File Organization**:

Use the app to sort images by date or folder to make it easier to locate specific files.

- **Delete After Transfer**:

    Enable the option to automatically delete files from the camera after transfer to free up storage.

Troubleshooting Common Issues

Transferring images via the Canon Camera Connect app is generally straightforward, but you may encounter occasional hiccups. Here are some common issues and how to resolve them:

- **Connection Drops During Transfer**:
    - Ensure your smartphone remains within range of the camera's Wi-Fi signal.
    - Avoid areas with heavy wireless interference.

- **App Fails to Detect the Camera**:
    - Restart both the app and the camera, then reconnect.
    - Make sure no other device is connected to the camera's Wi-Fi network.

- **Slow Transfer Speeds**:

    Large files like RAW images may take longer to transfer. For faster results, transfer smaller JPEG files.

- **Insufficient Storage on Device**:

    Check your smartphone's storage and clear unnecessary files if needed.

- **Error Messages on the Camera**:

    Update the camera's firmware and ensure the app is running the latest version.

Practical Use Cases for Image Transfer

For Beginners:

- Instantly share travel photos or family moments with friends and family.
- Use the app to organize your images into albums for easy access.

For Professionals:

- Send high-resolution images to clients in real time, especially during events.
- Transfer RAW files to your tablet for editing on the go using advanced editing software.

For Content Creators:

Streamline your workflow by moving images to your smartphone for immediate uploads to social media platforms like Instagram or YouTube thumbnails.

Tips for a Smoother Transfer Experience

- **Use a Dedicated Device:**

  For professional work, consider using a tablet with larger storage and better file-handling capabilities.

- **Keep Firmware Updated:**

  Regularly update your camera and app to ensure compatibility and access to new features.

- **Optimize File Organization:**

  Create specific folders in the app to categorize images, making it easier to locate and share files.

- **Use Resized Files for Social Media:**

  Transfer smaller, resized JPEGs to quickly upload to social media without compromising quality.

- **Transfer During Downtime:**

  Perform bulk transfers during breaks to avoid interruptions in your shooting workflow.

Conclusion

The Canon Camera Connect app is a game-changer for transferring images from your Canon EOS R5 Mark II to your smartphone or tablet. By understanding the setup process, customizing transfer settings, and troubleshooting common issues, you can unlock the full potential of wireless image transfer. Whether you're a beginner sharing family photos or a professional delivering high-resolution images to clients, the app provides a seamless and efficient solution for managing your files on the go.

Cloud Storage and Image Sharing Options

In today's digital world, cloud storage and image-sharing platforms have revolutionized the way photographers and videographers handle their media. The Canon EOS R5 Mark II, with its advanced connectivity features, allows users to seamlessly upload images and videos to the cloud or share them with others. This functionality is particularly beneficial for both beginners seeking a simple way to store and share their work and professionals who need efficient tools to manage and deliver their content.

What is Cloud Storage and Why Use It?

Cloud storage refers to a digital service where your data, including photos and videos, is saved on remote servers accessible via the internet. Instead of relying solely on physical storage like SD cards or hard drives, cloud services provide a secure, scalable, and convenient solution for storing media.

Key Benefits of Cloud Storage:

- **Backup and Security**:

    Protects your images from loss due to hardware failure, theft, or accidental deletion.

- **Accessibility**:

    Access your files anytime, anywhere, from any internet-connected device.

- **Collaboration**:

    Share files with clients or collaborators instantly without needing physical transfers.

- **Scalability**:

    Increase your storage capacity without investing in additional hardware.

- **Integration with Devices**:

    Many cloud platforms are compatible with Canon's ecosystem, streamlining the workflow.

Popular Cloud Storage Platforms for Canon EOS R5 Mark II Users

Here are some widely used platforms and their key features, suitable for photographers and videographers:

1. Canon image.canon

Canon's proprietary cloud service offers seamless integration with the EOS R5 Mark II.

- **Features**:
    - Auto-upload from the camera for files up to 10GB.
    - Temporary 30-day storage for original files before needing manual transfer to long-term storage.

- Direct integration with other services like Google Drive, Adobe Creative Cloud, and Microsoft OneDrive.

- **How to Use**:
    - Connect your camera to Wi-Fi.
    - Register your camera with image.canon through the Canon Camera Connect app.
    - Enable auto-upload to transfer images to the cloud after each shoot.

2. Google Drive

A widely used service for general file storage and sharing.

- **Features**:
    - Free 15GB storage with paid plans for additional capacity.
    - Easy sharing links for collaboration.
    - Supports viewing and basic editing of JPEG and HEIF files.

- **How to Use**:
    - Transfer files to your smartphone via the Canon Camera Connect app.
    - Upload the files to Google Drive using the mobile or web application.
    - Organize images into folders for easier management.

3. Adobe Creative Cloud

Designed for professionals who use Adobe's suite of photo and video editing tools.

- **Features**:
    - Integration with Lightroom and Photoshop.
    - Cloud editing and syncing across devices.
    - 1TB of storage with most Creative Cloud plans.

- **How to Use**:
    - Import images to Lightroom via the Canon Camera Connect app or computer.
    - Enable cloud sync to upload your edits and originals to Adobe's cloud.

4. Dropbox

A versatile platform with strong collaboration features.

- **Features**:
    - Easy sharing of large files and folders.
    - Automated backups for connected devices.
    - Offline access to synced files.
- **How to Use**:
    - Upload images via the mobile app or desktop application.
    - Share files using links or invitations.
    - Use the offline feature for accessing critical files during shoots.

5. SmugMug and Flickr

These platforms are tailored for photographers looking to showcase and share their work.

- **Features**:
    - High-quality photo storage.
    - Portfolio creation and public sharing.
    - Privacy settings for restricted viewing.
- **How to Use**:
    - Upload images directly from your smartphone or computer.
    - Use the app to organize galleries and customize your portfolio.

Image Sharing Options for Beginners and Professionals

Sharing images effectively is just as important as storing them. The EOS R5 Mark II's wireless capabilities make it simple to share images instantly.

1. Social Media Sharing

Platforms like Instagram, Facebook, and Twitter are ideal for reaching a broad audience.

- **Best Practices**:
    - Transfer smaller, resized JPEG files for faster uploads.
    - Add watermarks to protect your work from unauthorized use.

2. Client Deliveries

Professional photographers can use services like WeTransfer or Dropbox to deliver files to clients.

> **How to Deliver**:
> - Export images in the required format and resolution.
> - Share the link with password protection for added security.

3. Collaboration Tools

Use platforms like Google Photos or Microsoft OneDrive to collaborate with team members or editors.

How to Transfer Images to Cloud Storage

Step 1: Connect Your Camera to Wi-Fi

Enable Wi-Fi on your EOS R5 Mark II and connect it to a reliable network.

Step 2: Sync with a Cloud Platform

- For Canon image.canon:
    - Log in to the platform via the Canon Camera Connect app.
    - Set the auto-upload feature to send files to the cloud directly after shooting.
- For third-party platforms:
    - Transfer files to your smartphone or computer first.
    - Upload to your chosen cloud service using their app or website.

Step 3: Organize Your Files

Create folders based on events, clients, or categories to keep your storage system tidy.

Step 4: Share Links or Access

Use sharing features in your cloud service to grant access to specific people.

Troubleshooting Common Issues with Cloud Storage

1. Upload Failures

- **Problem**: Files fail to upload due to connectivity issues.

- **Solution**: Ensure you're connected to a stable Wi-Fi network and try uploading smaller batches.

2. Insufficient Storage Space

- **Problem**: Your cloud storage is full.
- **Solution**: Upgrade your plan or archive older files to an external hard drive.

3. Slow Upload Speeds

- **Problem**: Large RAW files take too long to upload.
- **Solution**: Resize files or use a wired connection to transfer them to a computer before uploading.

4. Access Issues

- **Problem**: Shared links don't work or recipients can't access files.
- **Solution**: Double-check privacy settings and ensure links are active.

Tips for Maximizing Cloud and Sharing Efficiency

- **Regular Backups**:

    Schedule automatic uploads to the cloud after each shoot to avoid manual transfers.

- **Use High-Speed Networks**:

    A strong Wi-Fi connection ensures faster uploads and fewer interruptions.

- **Leverage Mobile Apps**:

    Manage your cloud storage directly from your smartphone for added convenience.

- **Keep Files Organized**:

    Consistent naming conventions and folder structures make it easier to locate files.

Conclusion

Cloud storage and image-sharing options enhance the functionality of the Canon EOS R5 Mark II, making it an indispensable tool for modern photographers and videographers. Whether you're a beginner safeguarding your memories or a professional delivering high-quality images to clients, these technologies provide unmatched convenience and reliability. By understanding how to use these platforms effectively, you can streamline your workflow, safeguard your files, and showcase your work effortlessly.

CHAPTER 10

MAINTENANCE AND TROUBLESHOOTING

Cleaning and Caring for Your Camera and Lenses

Proper maintenance is essential to ensure the Canon EOS R5 Mark II delivers exceptional performance and lasts for years. Cameras are precision tools that require careful handling, and this is especially true for advanced models like the R5 Mark II. Dust, dirt, smudges, and fingerprints can degrade image quality and potentially harm the camera's sensitive components.

This section provides a detailed guide to cleaning and caring for your camera and lenses, ensuring they remain in optimal condition. Let's break this down into essential concepts and steps.

Why Cleaning and Caring Matter

- **Preserving Image Quality**: Dust on the sensor or fingerprints on the lens can cause blurry or spotty images. Regular cleaning ensures your images are crisp and clear.

- **Extending the Camera's Lifespan**: Keeping the camera body and lens clean prevents long-term damage from dirt or moisture.

- **Avoiding Costly Repairs**: Neglected cameras may need professional servicing, which can be expensive and time-consuming.

- **Ensuring Reliability in the Field**: A well-maintained camera is less likely to malfunction during critical shoots.

Cleaning Your Canon EOS R5 Mark II Camera

1. Cleaning the Camera Body

The camera body houses delicate electronics, so careful cleaning is necessary to avoid causing damage.

Tools You'll Need:

- Microfiber cloth
- Soft-bristled brush
- Lens cleaning blower
- Isopropyl alcohol (70% concentration) or specialized camera cleaning solution

Process:

- **Turn Off the Camera and Remove the Battery**: Always power down the camera and remove the battery before cleaning to avoid short circuits.
- **Dust Removal**: Use a soft-bristled brush to gently sweep dust from the body. For hard-to-reach areas, a lens cleaning blower can dislodge particles without contact.
- **Wiping the Exterior**: Use a microfiber cloth lightly dampened with isopropyl alcohol to wipe the camera body. Pay attention to areas around buttons and dials, where dirt often accumulates.
- **Check the Ports**: Inspect the ports (HDMI, USB, and headphone jack) and gently blow away any dust. Keep port covers closed when not in use to prevent buildup.

Pro Tip: Avoid using household cleaning agents, as they may damage the camera's surface or leave residues.

2. Cleaning the Lens

The lens is a critical part of the camera system, and any smudges or dust can directly impact the image quality.

Tools You'll Need:

- Lens cleaning solution
- Lens tissues or a microfiber lens cloth
- Lens blower
- Lens cleaning pen

Process:

- **Dust Removal**: Start with a lens blower to remove loose dust particles. Avoid using your breath, as moisture from it can create smudges.
- **Cleaning the Glass Surface**: Apply a few drops of lens cleaning solution to a microfiber cloth (never directly on the lens). Gently clean the lens surface in a circular motion, starting from the center and moving outward.
- **Edge Cleaning**: Use a lens cleaning pen to reach the edges of the lens. The soft tip is ideal for this purpose and won't scratch the glass.
- **Inspect the Lens**: Hold the lens up to the light to check for any remaining smudges or streaks. Repeat the cleaning if necessary.

Pro Tip: Always use lens caps when the lens is not in use to protect it from dirt and scratches.

3. Cleaning the Sensor

The Canon EOS R5 Mark II features a sophisticated sensor, which is prone to attracting dust during lens changes. Cleaning the sensor is delicate work and should be approached cautiously.

Tools You'll Need:

- Sensor cleaning swab (matched to the sensor size)
- Sensor cleaning solution
- Air blower

Process:

- **Activate the Sensor Cleaning Mode**: The R5 Mark II has an automated sensor cleaning feature that vibrates the sensor to dislodge dust. Access this from the menu before manual cleaning.
- **Use an Air Blower**: Hold the camera with the lens mount facing down and gently blow air onto the sensor to remove loose particles.
- **Manual Cleaning**: If dust remains, use a sensor cleaning swab. Add a small amount of sensor cleaning solution to the swab and gently swipe across the sensor in one direction. Use a fresh swab for additional passes.
- **Reassemble and Test**: Attach the lens, take a test photo, and check for any remaining spots.

Pro Tip: If you're unsure about cleaning the sensor yourself, seek professional cleaning services to avoid accidental damage.

Caring for Your Canon EOS R5 Mark II

1. Proper Storage

Storing your camera and lenses properly is as important as cleaning them.

Best Practices:

- **Use a Camera Bag**: Invest in a padded, weather-resistant camera bag to protect your gear from dust, moisture, and impact.
- **Store with Silica Gel Packs**: These absorb moisture and prevent fungus growth on lenses.
- **Avoid Direct Sunlight**: Store the camera in a cool, dry place away from direct sunlight, which can degrade materials over time.

2. Protecting Against Environmental Hazards

Outdoor photography exposes your camera to dust, water, and extreme temperatures. Taking precautions can prevent damage.

Tips:

- **Use a Protective Cover**: When shooting in dusty or rainy conditions, use a camera rain cover or weather-sealed housing.
- **Avoid Temperature Extremes**: Sudden temperature changes can cause condensation inside the camera. Gradually acclimate your gear when moving between environments.

3. Routine Inspections

Regularly inspect your camera and lenses for signs of wear or damage.

What to Check:

- **Camera Body**: Look for loose screws, dirt around dials, or damage to the LCD screen.
- **Lens Mount**: Ensure the lens mount is free of debris to maintain a secure fit and prevent scratches.
- **Lens Elements**: Check for scratches, cracks, or internal fogging.

Common Mistakes to Avoid

- **Using Canned Air**: The high pressure can force dirt deeper into the camera or leave a residue.
- **Touching the Sensor**: Sensors are delicate and can be easily scratched or damaged. Use only specialized tools for cleaning.
- **Skipping Lens Caps**: Leaving lenses uncapped increases the risk of scratches and dust buildup.
- **Overusing Cleaning Solutions**: Excess liquid can seep into the camera or lens and cause internal damage.

Establishing a Cleaning Routine

For best results, clean your camera and lenses regularly, especially after shooting in harsh environments.

- **Weekly Maintenance**: Dust off the camera body and clean the lens.

- **Monthly Maintenance**: Inspect and clean the sensor (if necessary) and check all camera components.
- **Post-Outdoor Shoots**: Perform a thorough cleaning to remove dirt and moisture.

Conclusion

Caring for your Canon EOS R5 Mark II and its lenses ensures consistently high performance and extends the life of your equipment. By following these simple yet essential cleaning steps, you'll protect your investment and enjoy hassle-free photography for years to come. Always handle your camera and lenses gently, use appropriate tools, and establish a regular maintenance routine to keep your gear in top condition.

Firmware Updates and Camera Calibration

Keeping your Canon EOS R5 Mark II in optimal working condition goes beyond regular cleaning. Firmware updates and camera calibration are critical maintenance tasks that ensure the camera operates efficiently, delivers consistent results, and keeps up with the latest technology and compatibility standards.

In this section, we will cover the importance of firmware updates, what camera calibration entails, and a step-by-step guide to performing these essential tasks. Whether you're a beginner or a professional, maintaining your camera's software and calibration can enhance your overall shooting experience.

Why Firmware Updates and Calibration Matter

- **Enhanced Performance**: Firmware updates improve camera functionality, fix bugs, and introduce new features. Calibration ensures accurate focusing and color reproduction.
- **Bug Fixes and Stability**: Updates resolve known issues, ensuring your camera operates smoothly under various conditions.
- **Compatibility**: Updates ensure your camera works seamlessly with new lenses, accessories, or software.
- **Precision and Accuracy**: Calibration adjusts the camera's systems to deliver sharp images and consistent colors, which is vital for professional-quality output.

Firmware Updates

What Is Firmware?

Firmware is the software embedded in your Canon EOS R5 Mark II that controls how the camera functions. Think of it as the operating system of your camera. Canon periodically releases firmware updates to improve performance, fix bugs, and add new features.

Key Benefits of Updating Firmware

- **Improved Autofocus**: Updates may enhance autofocus performance or add support for new autofocus modes.

- **New Features**: Firmware updates can introduce new creative tools, such as additional shooting modes or compatibility with updated lens technology.

- **Bug Fixes**: Errors or glitches reported by users are resolved through updates.

- **Compatibility Improvements**: Updates ensure compatibility with newly released lenses, memory cards, or third-party accessories.

How to Check and Update Firmware

Updating firmware is a straightforward process. Here's a step-by-step guide:

Tools You'll Need:

- A fully charged camera battery
- A memory card (formatted in the camera)
- A computer with internet access

Process:

1. **Check Your Current Firmware Version**:
    - Turn on your camera and access the menu.
    - Navigate to the *Firmware Version* option under the *Settings* tab. Note the current version.

2. **Visit Canon's Website**:
    - Go to the official Canon website and find the support page for the Canon EOS R5 Mark II.
    - Locate the *Firmware Updates* section and compare the latest version available with your camera's version.

3. **Download the Firmware File**:
    - If an update is available, download the firmware file to your computer.
    - Extract the downloaded file if it's in a compressed format (e.g., ZIP).

4. **Transfer the File to Your Memory Card**:

- Insert the formatted memory card into your computer and copy the firmware file onto the card.
- Do not place the file inside any folders on the card; it should be in the root directory.

5. **Insert the Card and Begin the Update**:
   - Insert the memory card into your camera.
   - Navigate to the *Firmware Version* option in the menu and select *Update Firmware*.
   - Follow the on-screen instructions to complete the update.

6. **Do Not Interrupt the Process**:

   Ensure the camera remains powered on during the update. Turning it off or removing the memory card during the process could damage the firmware.

7. **Verify the Update**:

   Once the update is complete, check the firmware version in the settings to confirm the update was successful.

Tips for Safe Firmware Updates

- **Use a Fully Charged Battery**: Running out of power during an update can corrupt the firmware.
- **Do Not Rush**: Follow each step carefully to avoid errors.
- **Download from Canon's Official Website**: Third-party websites may provide outdated or malicious files.

Camera Calibration

What Is Camera Calibration?

Camera calibration ensures the Canon EOS R5 Mark II performs at its best by fine-tuning critical systems like autofocus and color reproduction. Calibration aligns the camera's internal components to deliver accurate and consistent results.

When Is Calibration Needed?

- **Focus Issues**: If your images are consistently blurry despite proper focus settings, calibration may be necessary.

- **Color Inconsistencies**: Calibration ensures that colors captured by your camera match real-world tones or industry standards.
- **Using Third-Party Lenses**: Non-Canon lenses may require fine-tuning for compatibility.
- **After Firmware Updates**: Sometimes, major firmware updates can slightly alter camera settings, requiring recalibration.

Types of Calibration

- **Autofocus Microadjustment**: Ensures your camera's focus system aligns perfectly with the attached lens.
- **White Balance Calibration**: Adjusts the camera's interpretation of colors for accurate reproduction.
- **Monitor Calibration (External)**: If you use external monitors for video recording, calibrating their settings ensures they display colors accurately.

How to Perform Autofocus Calibration

Tools You'll Need:

- A calibration target (e.g., a printed chart or specialized tool like the Datacolor SpyderLensCal)
- A tripod
- Good lighting conditions

Process:

- **Set Up the Calibration Target**:

    Place the target on a flat surface with sufficient light. Ensure it's parallel to the camera sensor.

- **Position the Camera**:

    Mount the camera on a tripod and align it with the target. The target should fill the frame's center.

- **Access Microadjustment Settings**:
    - Navigate to the *AF Microadjustment* setting in the camera menu.
    - Follow the on-screen instructions to make adjustments.

- **Test and Adjust**:
    - Capture test shots and check the sharpness of the image.
    - Make incremental adjustments and repeat until the focus is accurate.
- **Save the Calibration**:

    Save the settings for the specific lens in the camera. If you use multiple lenses, repeat the process for each one.

How to Perform White Balance Calibration

Tools You'll Need:

A gray card or white balance calibration tool

Process:

- **Set Up the Gray Card**:

    Place the gray card in the same lighting conditions as your subject.

- **Capture a Reference Shot**:

    Take a photo of the gray card, ensuring it fills most of the frame.

- **Set Custom White Balance**:
    - Access the *Custom White Balance* setting in the menu.
    - Select the reference shot to apply the white balance.
- **Test the Results**:

    Capture additional shots and review the colors to ensure accuracy.

How to Calibrate an External Monitor

For video professionals using external monitors, calibration ensures consistent color grading.

Tools You'll Need:

A monitor calibration tool, such as the X-Rite i1Display Pro

Process:

- **Connect the Monitor**:

    Connect the external monitor to your Canon EOS R5 Mark II using an HDMI cable.

- **Run the Calibration Tool**:
    - Follow the instructions provided with the calibration tool.
    - Adjust brightness, contrast, and color settings as directed.
- **Save the Profile**:

    Save the calibration profile for future use.

Tips for Effective Calibration

- **Use Proper Lighting**: Calibrate under the lighting conditions in which you'll be shooting.
- **Document Your Settings**: Keep a record of your adjustments for future reference.
- **Recalibrate Periodically**: Regular recalibration ensures consistent performance over time.

Conclusion

Firmware updates and camera calibration are indispensable for maintaining the Canon EOS R5 Mark II. Firmware updates keep the camera up to date with the latest features, resolve bugs, and improve compatibility, while calibration fine-tunes the camera's systems for optimal performance. Whether you're updating your firmware or calibrating your autofocus, following these steps ensures your camera operates at its best, delivering reliable results for both beginners and professionals.

Troubleshooting Common Issues and Errors

Even with a sophisticated and reliable camera like the Canon EOS R5 Mark II, occasional problems can arise. Whether you're a beginner or a professional, understanding common issues and knowing how to address them can save time, effort, and stress. This section explains how to troubleshoot frequent errors and camera problems effectively.

Why Troubleshooting is Essential

- **Avoid Downtime**: Quick fixes can prevent interruptions during important shoots.
- **Save Money**: Many issues can be resolved without the need for professional repairs.
- **Enhance Confidence**: Familiarity with troubleshooting builds trust in your camera's capabilities.

Common Issues and Their Solutions

1. Camera Won't Turn On

A non-responsive camera is one of the most frustrating problems. The issue could be as simple as a dead battery or as complex as a hardware malfunction.

Steps to Troubleshoot:

- **Check the Battery**:
    - Ensure the battery is charged. Insert a fully charged battery into the camera.
    - Inspect the battery terminals for dirt or corrosion. Clean them gently with a dry cloth if needed.

- **Test the Power Switch**:

    Make sure the power switch is fully toggled to the *On* position.

- **Inspect the Battery Compartment**:

    Look for obstructions, debris, or damaged contacts.

- **Reset the Camera**:

    Remove the battery and memory card, wait a few minutes, and reinsert them. This can clear temporary glitches.

- **Contact Support**:

    If the camera still won't power on, it may require professional servicing.

2. Lens Won't Attach or Detach

Difficulty attaching or detaching a lens can occur due to misalignment, debris, or a damaged mount.

Steps to Troubleshoot:

- **Check the Lens Mount**:

    Ensure the lens and camera mounts are clean. Dust or dirt can block proper attachment. Use a blower to remove particles.

- **Align the Lens Correctly**:

    Match the alignment marks on the lens and the camera body before rotating the lens into place.

- **Inspect for Damage**:

Look for bent or damaged metal contacts on the lens or camera mount.

- **Use Gentle Force**:

    Avoid forcing the lens into place, as this can cause further damage. If it doesn't attach smoothly, stop and reassess the issue.

3. Blurry Images

Blurry photos can result from focus issues, camera shake, or incorrect settings.

Steps to Troubleshoot:

- **Check the Focus Mode**:

    Ensure the autofocus (AF) is enabled if you're not using manual focus.

- **Stabilize the Camera**:

    Use a tripod or enable in-body image stabilization (IBIS) for handheld shots.

- **Increase Shutter Speed**:

    A slow shutter speed can cause motion blur. Increase the shutter speed for fast-moving subjects.

- **Clean the Lens**:

    Smudges or dirt on the lens can reduce image sharpness. Follow proper lens cleaning techniques to resolve this.

- **Inspect Autofocus Settings**:

    Ensure the correct AF mode is selected, such as *One Shot* for still subjects or *Servo AF* for moving ones.

4. Memory Card Errors

Errors such as "Card Not Recognized" or "Card Full" can disrupt your workflow.

Steps to Troubleshoot:

- **Format the Card**:

    If the card is new or has been used in another device, format it using the camera's menu system to ensure compatibility.

- **Check Card Compatibility**:

Use memory cards recommended for the R5 Mark II. Look for high-speed SD or CFexpress cards that meet Canon's specifications.

- **Inspect the Card Slot**:

  Check for dust or damage in the memory card slot. Use a blower to remove debris gently.

- **Try Another Card**:

  Insert a different card to determine if the issue is with the card or the camera.

- **Backup and Replace**:

  If the card is repeatedly causing errors, back up your data and replace the card.

5. Overheating During Extended Use

The R5 Mark II is capable of recording high-resolution video, which can cause the camera to overheat during long sessions.

Steps to Troubleshoot:

- **Monitor Usage**:

  Take breaks between extended video recording sessions to allow the camera to cool down.

- **Use External Accessories**:

  Attach an external cooling fan or use an external recorder to reduce internal processing.

- **Lower Video Settings**:

  Reduce resolution or frame rate to decrease heat generation.

- **Improve Ventilation**:

  Avoid using the camera in direct sunlight or enclosed spaces.

- **Enable Overheat Control**:

  Activate the *Overheat Control* setting in the menu to limit overheating automatically.

6. Connectivity Issues with Wi-Fi or Bluetooth

Wireless connectivity problems can interfere with remote control or file transfers.

Steps to Troubleshoot:

- **Check Settings**:

    Ensure Wi-Fi and Bluetooth are enabled in the camera menu.

- **Reconnect Devices**:

    Delete the existing pairing and reconnect your smartphone or computer.

- **Update Software**:

    Ensure the Canon Camera Connect app and camera firmware are up to date.

- **Test in a Low-Interference Area**:

    Avoid crowded networks, as they can cause interference.

7. Error Messages on the Screen

Error codes or messages like "Err 01" or "Err 70" indicate specific issues.

Steps to Troubleshoot:

- **Refer to the Manual**:

    Check the error code in the camera's user manual or Canon's support website for guidance.

- **Reset the Camera**:

    Turn off the camera, remove the battery, and reinsert it after a few minutes.

- **Inspect Connections**:

    Errors may occur due to poor contact between the lens and camera body. Clean the contacts gently.

- **Update Firmware**:

    Firmware updates often resolve error-related bugs.

- **Seek Professional Help**:

    Persistent errors may indicate hardware problems that require servicing.

8. Battery Drains Quickly

Short battery life can disrupt long shoots.

Steps to Troubleshoot:

- **Use a Genuine Battery**:

  Non-Canon batteries may not provide optimal performance.

- **Check Background Features**:

  Turn off features like Wi-Fi, Bluetooth, or image stabilization when not needed.

- **Lower Screen Brightness**:

  Reduce the LCD screen brightness to conserve power.

- **Carry Spares**:

  Always have a fully charged spare battery on hand.

- **Inspect for Faults**:

  If a battery drains unusually fast, it may need replacement.

General Tips for Troubleshooting

- **Regular Maintenance**:

  Clean your camera and lenses regularly to prevent many issues from occurring.

- **Stay Updated**:

  Keep firmware up to date to benefit from the latest improvements and fixes.

- **Back Up Settings**:

  Save custom settings to restore them if the camera needs to be reset.

- **Know When to Seek Help**:

If troubleshooting doesn't resolve the issue, consult Canon support or visit an authorized service center.

Conclusion

Troubleshooting is an essential skill for any photographer or videographer. By understanding and addressing common issues like power problems, focus errors, and connectivity glitches, you can keep your Canon EOS R5 Mark II performing at its best. With these practical solutions, you'll spend less time fixing issues and more time creating stunning images and videos.

GLOSSARY

AEB (Auto Exposure Bracketing)

A feature that captures multiple shots at different exposures to ensure one is perfectly exposed. This is useful in tricky lighting conditions or for creating HDR images.

AF (Autofocus)

The camera's system for automatically focusing on a subject. The EOS R5 Mark II offers advanced Dual Pixel Autofocus, enabling fast and accurate subject tracking.

Aperture

The adjustable opening in a lens that controls the amount of light reaching the camera sensor. Aperture is measured in f-stops (e.g., f/2.8, f/5.6), with lower numbers representing wider openings.

Aspect Ratio

The ratio of an image's width to its height. Common aspect ratios include 3:2 (used in DSLR and mirrorless cameras) and 16:9 (used in widescreen videos).

Bit Depth

The amount of color and tonal information in an image. Higher bit depths, like 10-bit or 12-bit, provide more flexibility for color grading and editing, especially in video files.

Burst Mode

A shooting mode that allows the camera to take multiple photos in rapid succession. Useful for capturing action or fast-moving subjects.

Buffer

The temporary memory in a camera that stores images before they are written to the memory card. A larger buffer allows for longer burst shooting, important in action and sports photography.

Cloud Storage

A digital service that stores your photos and videos online, providing easy access and backup. Popular platforms include Canon's image.canon, Google Drive, and Dropbox.

Crop Factor

The ratio of a camera sensor's size to a full-frame sensor. While the EOS R5 Mark II is a full-frame camera, crop sensors reduce the effective field of view of a lens, making a 50mm lens behave like an 80mm lens on a 1.6x crop sensor.

Depth of Field (DOF)

The range of focus in an image, controlled by aperture, focal length, and distance from the subject. A shallow depth of field creates a blurred background, while a deep depth of field keeps more of the image in focus.

Dual Pixel Autofocus (DPAF)

Canon's advanced autofocus technology, where each pixel on the sensor is split into two, allowing precise and fast focusing during still photography and video. The R5 Mark II uses an improved version of this technology for better subject tracking.

EVF (Electronic Viewfinder)

A small digital display that replicates the scene as seen through the camera lens, showing exposure, color, and settings in real-time. The EOS R5 Mark II features a high-resolution EVF for accurate composition.

Exposure Compensation

A setting that allows you to manually adjust the brightness of an image by overriding the camera's metering system. It is measured in stops, such as +1.0 or -1.0.

Exposure Triangle

The three key settings—ISO, aperture, and shutter speed—that work together to determine the brightness of an image. Understanding this concept is essential for mastering manual photography.

Field of View (FOV)

The visible area captured by the camera, determined by the lens and sensor size. Wide-angle lenses provide a large field of view, while telephoto lenses focus on narrower portions of the scene.

Firmware
The software that operates your camera. Keeping firmware updated ensures optimal performance, access to new features, and fixes for known issues.

Flash Sync Speed

The fastest shutter speed at which a camera can synchronize with a flash. Using a shutter speed faster than this can result in part of the image being dark due to the shutter blocking the flash.

Focal Length

The distance (in millimeters) from the lens to the camera sensor when the subject is in focus. It determines the angle of view, with shorter focal lengths providing a wider angle and longer focal lengths offering greater zoom.

Focus Peaking

A feature that highlights the areas in focus on the camera's display or EVF, making manual focusing easier and more precise.

Histogram Clipping

Occurs when parts of the histogram are pushed off the edges, indicating that details are lost in the shadows (black clipping) or highlights (white clipping). Clipping should generally be avoided for well-exposed photos.

Intervalometer

A tool or camera feature that takes photos at preset intervals. It is useful for time-lapse photography, letting the camera automatically capture a sequence of images over time.

ISO (International Standards Organization)

A camera setting that controls the sensor's sensitivity to light. Lower ISO values (e.g., 100) produce less noise, while higher values (e.g., 3200) are useful in low-light situations but can increase noise.

Keystone Distortion

A type of distortion that occurs when a subject is photographed at an angle, making straight lines appear slanted. It is common in architectural photography and can be corrected in editing software.

Lens Flare

The unwanted glare or artifacts caused when bright light, like the sun, directly hits the lens. Using a lens hood or adjusting the angle can reduce flare.

Low-Pass Filter

A component in some camera sensors that reduces moiré patterns (unwanted interference effects) by slightly blurring fine details. The EOS R5 Mark II uses advanced sensor design to minimize the need for such filters.

Manual Focus (MF)

A focusing method where the photographer adjusts the lens manually instead of relying on the camera's autofocus system. Manual focus is ideal for precise control in situations where autofocus may struggle, like macro photography.

Overexposure

When too much light hits the camera sensor, causing parts of an image to appear overly bright or "blown out," with loss of detail in the highlights. Adjusting exposure settings or using exposure compensation can fix this.

Pixel Pitch

The distance between pixels on a camera sensor. Smaller pixel pitch generally means more pixels on a sensor but can result in more noise, particularly in low light.

Prime Lens

A lens with a fixed focal length, such as 50mm or 85mm. Prime lenses often have wider apertures and produce sharper images compared to zoom lenses.

Remote Shooting

Controlling the camera remotely using an app or dedicated remote control device. With the Canon Camera Connect app, users can adjust settings and capture images without touching the camera.

Sensor Cleaning

The process of removing dust and debris from the camera sensor. The EOS R5 Mark II includes an automatic sensor cleaning feature to reduce maintenance needs.

Shutter Lag

The delay between pressing the shutter button and the photo being captured. High-end cameras like the EOS R5 Mark II minimize shutter lag for responsive shooting.

Tethered Shooting

A technique where the camera is connected to a computer or tablet for direct image transfer and live view. This is popular in studio settings for real-time image review.

Underexposure

When too little light reaches the camera sensor, causing the image to appear dark and lack detail in the shadows. Adjusting the exposure or increasing the ISO can help balance this.

White Balance

A camera setting that adjusts colors to appear natural under different lighting conditions. Presets include daylight, tungsten, and fluorescent, while manual options allow for custom adjustments.

Zoom Lens

A lens with variable focal lengths, allowing you to zoom in or out without changing the lens. For example, a 24-70mm zoom lens can cover wide-angle to short telephoto ranges. Zoom lenses are versatile and popular for various types of photography.

www.ingramcontent.com/pod-product-compliance
Lightning Source LLC
Chambersburg PA
CBHW082247220526
45469CB00009B/2910